Hawthorne Revisited

Honoring the Bicentennial of the Author's Birth

A collection of essays assembled by Gordon Hyatt
Project Director, The Hawthorne Bicentennial

Publication conceived by Gordon Hyatt
Edited by David Scribner
Original cut-paper illustrations by Pamela Dalton
Cover, book design, and typesetting by Jane McWhorter, Blue Sky Productions.

Front cover (dust jacket): Painting by Emanuel Gottlieb Leutze, National Portrait Gallery, Smithsonian Institution; transfer from the National Gallery of Art; gift of Andrew W. Mellon, 1942.

Rear cover (dust jacket): Sculpture by Daniel Chester French. Chesterwood, a National Trust Historic Site, Stockbridge, MA. Photograph by De Witt Ward.

Library of Congress Card Catalog Number: 1-58465-374-4

Underwritten by Grants from:
Berkshire Bank Foundation, The Gilder Lehrman Institute of American History, The Lehrman Foundation, The High Meadow Foundation, Furthermore: a program of the J. M. Kaplan Fund.

Lenox Library Association
18 Main Street
Lenox, MA 01240
Denis Lesieur, Executive Director

Hawthorne Revisited

Honoring the Bicentennial of the Author's Birth

By Louis Auchincloss • Paul Auster • Laura L. Butters
M. Gerard Fromm • Wendell Garrett • Carol Gilligan
Michael T. Gilmore • Elizabeth Hardwick • Harrison Hayford
Neil Hickey • Alexandria Mason • Hershel Parker • Peggy Strong
Tom Wicker • Brenda Wineapple

Edited by David Scribner
Original Cut-Paper Illustrations by Pamela Dalton
Executive Editor & Project Director Gordon Hyatt

Published by Lenox Library Association
Lenox, Massachusetts

Distributed by University Press of New England
Hanover, New Hampshire, and London

"... there seems to be no way but to go on winning victories, and establishing peace and truer union in another generation, at the expense, probably, of greater trouble, in the present one, than any other people voluntarily suffered."
— Nathaniel Hawthorne, 1862

Bust of Nathaniel Hawthorne by Maria Louise Lander

Miss Lander, originally from Salem, was a part of the colony of American artists living in Rome where the Hawthornes met her. A free-living spirit, she served, in part, as the inspiration for Hilda, a character in Hawthorne's last novel, The Marble Faun. *The bust was retouched to the point where son Julian complained that it looked like "a combination of Daniel Webster and George Washington."*

Contents

Preface
Notes On Berkshire County

Nathaniel Hawthorne is often called "the Salem author" but we in the Berkshires owe him a historic debt, too, for although he spent only a year and a half in the Berkshires, from May 1850 to November 1851, his presence has remained a powerful influence on this region.

These western hills have long been an area where artistic and literary imaginations have flourished alongside agriculture, industry and what is now termed "cultural tourism." In the mid-19th century, when both Nathaniel Hawthorne and Herman Melville were writing classics of American literature within a few miles of each other, (*The House of the Seven Gables* in Lenox by Hawthorne and *Moby-Dick* in Pittsfield by Melville) there was no wide audience, nor dependable fiscal support, for American literature. Melville came here from New York City to escape the "brick kiln" heat of summer; Hawthorne came here from Salem to escape the political heat surrounding his dismissal from the U.S. Custom House.

The Berkshires' pastoral beauty clearly comforted each of them: Hawthorne praised the view from his little red cottage across the fields to Stockbridge Bowl, an area he named "Tanglewood"; Melville drew inspiration from the snow-covered whale-like form of Mount Greylock to the north of his study window. In the same era, a grand theatrical flair was added with the unavoidable presence of the English actress, Fanny Kemble; rhyme with reason flowed from the pen of Oliver Wendell Holmes; and

Henry Wadsworth Longfellow married Fanny Appleton from Pittsfield. Such figures gave the area its early reputation as "the American lake district" after the vacation county in England where Wordsworth had flourished — and this encouraged others to follow.

The pastoral qualities of the hills belied a vigorous agricultural and industrial prosperity. Paper mills had been founded here beginning in 1799. An 1837 census enumerated 136,962 sheep dotting the Berkshires clearcut fields whose trees had been reduced to charcoal to smelt iron. Here was spun wool for the Union army and by 1875 the woolen industry comprised 50 percent of the Berkshire economy. Electrical, plastic and defense manufacturing were to follow. While these diverse industries sustained the local population, the county's natural attraction to creative people expanded to include a new, wealthy class.

By the turn of the century, when sculptor Daniel Chester French had established Chesterwood, his studio in Glendale section of Stockbridge, upwards of seventy-five major estates had been built here, bringing the Gilded Age solidly to the Berkshire hills. At the same time the arts in America grew and prospered. In 1900, when Edith Wharton established herself at The Mount in Lenox, American literature as a profession had arrived; Mrs. Wharton herself was the highest paid writer of her time.

The reputation of the Berkshires as a place for those seeking solace in the cooler hills led to burgeoning Berkshire businesses and a wide variety of resort facilities — hotels with wide porches, homes making beds and breakfasts, farmsteads converted to country places, cottages lining the lakesides, estates transformed into museums, hotels and spas. Summer people were now an important factor in the annual economy, attracted to performing institutions like Tanglewood, the Berkshire Playhouse (now the Berkshire Theatre Festival), Jacob's Pillow Dance Festival, Shakespeare & Company, the Massachusetts Museum of Contemporary Art, the Clark Art Institute, the Williamstown Theatre Festival, as well as art and sports camps for the youngsters.

The Berkshire Visitors Bureau proclaims the region to be America's "Premier Cultural Resort." We owe this apt description to the accomplishments of authors like Nathaniel Hawthorne, Herman Melville, and Edith Wharton and also to the writers, artists and composers who followed and who continue to find the Berkshires extraordinarily hospitable to the active imagination.

Introduction

By Gordon Hyatt

In 2004, the bicentennial of Nathaniel Hawthorne's birth, many individuals and organizations will celebrate the author. He will be honored with readings of his works, a conference of The Hawthorne Society in Salem, exhibitions and concerts, symposiums, radio readings of his short stories. and discussion seminars planned for Massachusetts, New York and beyond.

Two of Hawthorne's productive years, 1850 and 1851, were spent out "West" — in Lenox, Berkshire County, Massachusetts. The Lenox Library offers this volume to commemorate those years.

Each of the writers who have generously contributed to this book shines contemporary perspective on Hawthorne's life, his works, his personality and his current influence on American literature. Disciplines represented include novelists, historians, scholars, curators, journalists, biographers, a psychologist, and a feminist/dramatist. Their articles fall into two basic categories: history and criticism. We also present the full text of Hawthorne's extraordinary report of 1862, *Chiefly About War Matters by a Peaceable Man.*

In 1904, the Hawthorne Centenary was celebrated at The Wayside in Concord, Massachusetts, the only home that Hawthorne ever owned. The proceedings commenced with the unveiling of a bronze tablet by his granddaughter Beatrix Hawthorne:

1904 Centenary Tablet

As the plaque above suggests, Hawthorne, a dedicated pedestrian, paced to and fro throughout his life — tramping the woods of Maine, the streets of Salem, the docks of Boston, the riverbanks of Concord, the fields and stables of Brook Farm, the dirt roads of the Berkshires, the squares of Liverpool, the hills of Rome, the marbled halls of Florence, the lanes of London, the Capitol corridors in Washington, the round-house at Harper's Ferry, the decks of sailing ships and warships, the floors of stately mansions, Custom houses, Shaker settlements, libraries, publishing houses, oyster bars and more — in sum, the walkways of his nineteenth-century world. He kept journals of these movements all of his life, journals that were to be published after his death. They were edited for polite sensibilities by his widow — and then published unaltered by the scholars who succeeded her. Still, knowing where Hawthorne had traveled does not make it easier to understand this seminal, quixotic, secretive, talented American original.

An aura of intense privacy surrounded Hawthorne's behavior, often confounding his contemporaries. Julia Ward Howe offered this memory in 1904:

> *More than fifty years ago Dr. Howe and I drove out to Concord to visit Horace Mann and his wife, (Sophia Hawthorne's sister), who had found a summer boarding place next door to the Manse, where the Hawthornes were installed. We brought with us our little*

daughter of about the same age as Una Hawthorne. In the course of the day, we found our way into the Hawthorne residence, where Mrs. Hawthorne received us very graciously. She promised that we should see her husband. Just then a male figure descended the stairs. "My husband," she cried, "here are Dr. and Mrs. Howe." What we did see was a broad hat pulled down over a hidden face, and a figure that quickly vanished through an opposite door."[1]

In 1846, in *Mosses from an Old Manse*, Hawthorne offered this much-quoted personal insight:

So far as I am a man of really individual attributes, I veil my face, nor am I, nor have ever been, one of those supremely hospitable people, who serve up their own hearts delicately fried, with brain-sauce, as a tidbit for their beloved public.

It would be unfair to characterize Hawthorne simply as a wizard posing behind the curtain of his privacy. He shared his deepest moments of creativity with the anonymous and (presumably) gentle readers in his audience, as here in "The Custom-House Introductory" to *The Scarlet Letter*:

Moonlight in a familiar room, falling so white upon the carpet, and showing all its figures so distinctly, — making every object so minutely visible, yet so unlike a morning or noontide visibility, — is a medium the most suitable for a romance-writer to get acquainted with his illusive guests. Thus, therefore, the floor of our familiar room has become a neutral territory, somewhere between the real world and fairy-land, where the Actual and the Imaginary may meet, and each imbue itself with the nature of the other. Ghosts might enter here, without affrighting us. . . . The somewhat dim coal-fire has an essential influence in producing the effect which I would describe. It throws its unobtrusive tinge throughout the room, with a faint ruddiness upon the walls and ceiling, and a reflected gleam from the polish of the furniture. . . . Glancing at the looking-glass, we behold — deep within its haunted verge — the smoldering glow of the half-extinguished anthracite, the white moonbeams on the floor, and a repetition of all the gleam and shadow of the picture, with one remove farther from the actual, and nearer to the imaginative. Then, at such an hour, and with this scene before him,

*if a man, sitting all alone, cannot dream strange things, and make
them look like truth, he need never try to write romances.*

Hawthorne trained himself to write — spending over a decade as a
reclusive apprentice in the upstairs room in the family house in Salem he
termed his "dismal chamber." He soon came to understand the financial
impossibility of earning a living from literature in mid-nineteenth
century America. Honest work in the custom service, secured through
political patronage, became his life support — natural for a man born in
a seaport village, renowned for the prosperity of its China trade.

Though Hawthorne is often termed "the Salem author," in honor of
his birthplace, many locales housed his years. At least six historic sites are
identified with his life and work. In Salem the U.S. Custom House where
he worked, his birthplace, and The House of the Seven Gables (with over
120,000 visitations annually) are key landmarks; in Concord visitors seek
out The Old Manse maintained by the Trustees of Reservations and The
Wayside, a property of the National Park Service; in the Berkshires a replica of the little red cottage stands on the grounds of Tanglewood, today
the site of the Boston Symphony Orchestra's summer music festival. It
was here that he wrote *The House of the Seven Gables, The Wonder Book
for Girls and Boys,* as well as his journal, including the recently published
Twenty Days with Julian & Little Bunny by Papa.

Here, too, Hawthorne developed his influential relationship with
Herman Melville — that began on what is often termed America's most
famous literary picnic. The two men hiked Monument Mountain in
Stockbridge with a number of companions. An attraction and friendship deepened over the dinner "well-moistened with wines" that concluded the day. Within a few weeks Melville moved to Pittsfield, about
six miles from Hawthorne and his family in Lenox. Both men were
simultaneously engaged intensely with writing, Hawthorne with *The
House of the Seven Gables,* Melville with *Moby-Dick.* Hawthorne created
his realistically detailed romance of Salem contemporaries haunted and
cursed by the deeds of their Colonial forbears while Melville wrote his
mythic epic of self-destructive obsession.

The extent of the landlocked older man's influence on seafaring
Melville is the subject of Harrison Hayford's 1945 dissertation, here
published for the first time. That Hawthorne understood Melville's

literary accomplishment is clearly reflected in his letters of passionate gratitude; that Hawthorne may have found the younger man too needy to endure may be seen in his abrupt departure from the Berkshires soon after the publication of *Moby-Dick; or, The Whale* with its dedication:

IN TOKEN

OF MY ADMIRATION FOR HIS GENIUS.

𝕿𝖍𝖎𝖘 𝕭𝖔𝖔𝖐 𝖎𝖘 𝕴𝖓𝖘𝖈𝖗𝖎𝖇𝖊𝖉

TO

NATHANIEL HAWTHORNE.

Two years later, after the two met for the last time, walking about Liverpool where Hawthorne was U.S. Consul from 1852-56, Hawthorne wrote this of Melville:

If he were a religious man, he would be one of the most truly religious and reverential; he has a very high and noble nature, and better worth immortality than most of us.

As we revisit Hawthorne during the bicentennial of his birth, we present five articles dealing with historical aspects of his life and times and world. Novelist Paul Auster discovers Hawthorne at home in the Berkshires and offers a clear perspective on the author's life at the height of his creative powers and domestic happiness. Americana expert and author Wendell Garrett takes us back to Salem, the author's native town, to describe the seaport's commercial rise and fall. Peggy Strong reviews the lives of the Peabody sisters; the youngest, Sophia, married Hawthorne. Laurie Butters, historic site manager of The Old Manse in Concord, describes Thoreau's contribution to the Hawthorne's first home: planting their kitchen garden — and what has evolved on the site today. The gabled house in Salem that Hawthorne made world-famous inspired him even as the fame of his novel inspired drastic changes to the house — chronicled by Alexandria Mason, curator at The House of the Seven Gables.

Revisiting Hawthorne confirms how history and his work are entwined — much of his writing is anchored in Massachusetts's Puritan past. The dark evils of earlier times that resound in his art have consistently inspired critical evaluation. The list of fellow authors drawn to interpret him began with Melville's remarkable 1850 essay *Hawthorne and his Mosses.* Melville chose a sailor's simile to describe Hawthorne's "great deep intellect, which drops down into the universe like a plummet," this man who is a member of a "new and far better generation" of American writers:

> For spite of all, the Indian-summer sunlight on the hither side
> of Hawthorne's soul, the other side — like the dark half of the
> physical sphere — is shrouded in a blackness, ten times black.

Melville's appraisal was followed by a pantheon of nineteenth-century literary notables commenting on Hawthorne's work: Edgar Allen Poe, Anthony Trollope, Oliver Wendell Holmes, D.H. Lawrence and Henry James. Twentieth-century scholars included Mark Van Doren and Van Wyck Brooks. By then, however, the host of critics, literary analysts and graduate students compelled to interpret Hawthorne was legion. Their numbers continue expanding in the twenty-first century. Our legion includes novelist Louis Auchincloss speculating on the gravity of adultery as a sin, and essayist and novelist Elizabeth Hardwick speculating both on Auchincloss and the theme of seduction and betrayal in *The Scarlet Letter.*

Our critical concerns shift to pragmatic choices with author and university professor Carol Gilligan's account of incorporating feminist themes when she dramatized *The Scarlet Letter.* Neil Hickey, a longtime media observer, reviewed several feature film interpretations of Hawthorne's masterpiece, finding the moral and social conflict of the novel slipping further and further from the more recent screenplays.

How did Hawthorne understand the dark elements in human nature? How did he know that Reverend Dimmesdale would develop his fatal psychosomatic illness stemming from his secret sin generations before Freud identified the syndrome? This is the first question addressed by clinical psychologist Gerard Fromm in an analysis that probes the known facts of Hawthorne's life. Michael Gilmore, a Hawthorne scholar, challenges the critical consensus that the author's works are testaments to inaction. Hawthorne biographer Brenda Wineapple, whose *Hawthorne,*

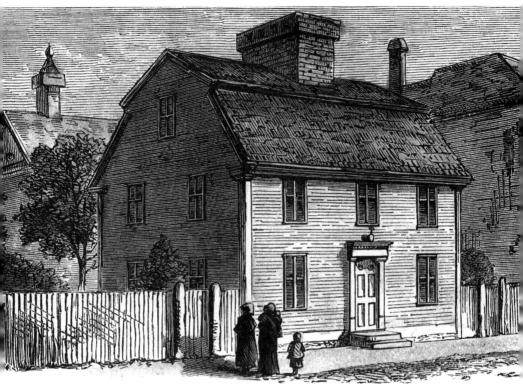

Hawthorne's birthplace, 27 Union Street, Salem. The house was moved to the Seven Gables Settlement Association site after the turn of the century.

A Life was published in 2003, finds contemporary relevance in the way that Hawthorne, a man of his times, envisioned an America "conceived in freedom and slavery." Politically, he sided with Franklin Pierce, the fourteenth president of the United States and with the Democratic Party's support of the Constitution, the document that institutionalized slavery as part of the American system. In his 1851 campaign biography. *The Life of Franklin Pierce,* Hawthorne endorsed his friend and patron's "opinions upon the slavery question which he has never since seen occasion to change in the slightest degree."

After Hawthorne completed his work as U.S. Consul in Liverpool, his grand tour to Italy and his last novel, *The Marble Faun,* he returned with his family to Concord, "In Advance of the General Ruin," as his biographer James R. Mellow called those times just before the Civil War. When war was declared, the ensuing months of indecisive results led Hawthorne to conclude the Union might have been better off if certain states were divested from the nation. In May 1861, he wrote to a friend: "We never were one people, and never really had a country since the Constitution was formed."

Hawthorne ultimately came directly to grips with wartime as an observer, a war correspondent. Accepting an assignment from The Atlantic Monthly, he made a remarkable foray to Washington and the front. His article, *Chiefly About War Matters* bylined *by a Peaceable Man,* appears in full in this volume. It is characterized by Mellow as giving "evidence as to the vigor of Hawthorne's style" and by Wineapple as "a *tour de force . . .* Swiftian, corrosive and funny, and directed at the foibles . . . of humankind."

Perhaps Hawthorne's closing line best reflects his feelings:

There are some degrees of absurdity that put Reason herself into a rage, and affect us like an intolerable crime. . . which this Rebellion is, into the bargain.

Veteran reporter, historian and novelist Tom Wicker's appraisal of Hawthorne's accomplishments brings a journalist's critical appreciation to this unprecedented example of Hawthorne's variety.

It is with these Bicentennial perspectives — revisiting Hawthorne, the "Salem author" known world wide — that we seek to celebrate, to honor and to understand this artist of American literature.

1. *The Hawthorne Centenary Celebration* (Houghton, Mifflin and Company, 1905), 37.

Hawthorne Revisited
HISTORY

"He happened to be one of the first great artisit in America; and he did not know how to be comfortable with the fact."

— Mark Van Doren, 1950

Hawthorne
at Home

Excerpted from the introduction to Nathaniel Hawthorne's
Twenty Days with Julian & Little Bunny by Papa

By Paul Auster

T*wenty Days with Julian & Little Bunny by Papa* is one of the least-known works by a well-known writer in all of literature. Buried in the seventh folio of Hawthorne's *American Notebooks* — that massive, little-read tome of treasures and revelations — the fifty pages that comprise this brief, self-contained narrative were written in Lenox, Massachusetts, between July 28 and August 16, 1851. In June of the previous year, Hawthorne and his wife had moved to a small red farmhouse in the Berkshires with their two children, Una (born in 1844) and Julian (born in 1846). A third child, Rose, was born in May 1851. A couple of months later, accompanied by her two daughters and her older sister, Elizabeth Peabody, Sophia Hawthorne left Lenox to visit her parents in West Newton, just outside Boston. Remaining in the house were Hawthorne, the five-year-old Julian, Mrs. Peters (the cook and housekeeper), and a pet rabbit that eventually came to be known as Hindlegs. That evening, after putting Julian to bed, Hawthorne sat down and wrote the first chapter of his little saga. With no intention other than to record the doings in the household during his wife's absence, he had inadvertently embarked on something that no writer had ever attempted before: a meticulous, blow-by-blow account of a man taking care of a young child by himself.

By the summer of 1851, Hawthorne was a seasoned observer of his own children, a veteran of family life. He was forty-seven years old and had been married for close to a decade. He couldn't have known it then, but nearly every important word of fiction he would ever publish had already been written. Behind him were the two editions of *Twice-Told Tales* (1837 and 1842), *Mosses from an Old Manse* (1846), and *The Snow-Image and Other Twice-Told Tales* (already finished and planned for publication in late 1851) — his entire output as a writer of short stories. His first two novels had been published in 1850 and 1851. *The Scarlet Letter* had turned "the obscurest man of letters in America" into one of the most respected and celebrated writers of his time, and *The House of the Seven Gables* had only strengthened his reputation, prompting many critics to call him the finest writer the Republic had yet produced. Years of solitary labor had at last won him public reward, and after two decades of scrambling to make ends meet, 1851 marked the first year that Hawthorne earned enough from his writing to be able to support his family. Nor was there any reason to think that his success would not continue. Throughout the spring and early summer, he had written *A Wonder Book for Girls and Boys,* finishing the preface on July 15, just two weeks before Sophia's departure for West Newton, and he was already making plans for his next novel, *The Blithedale Romance.* Looking back on Hawthorne's career now, and knowing that he would be dead just thirteen years later (a few weeks short of his sixtieth birthday), that season in Lenox stands out as one of the happiest periods of his life, a moment of sublime equipoise and fulfillment. But it was nearly August now, and for many years Hawthorne had routinely suspended his literary work during the hot months. It was a time for loafing and reflection, in his opinion, a time for being outdoors, and he had always written as little as possible throughout the dog days of the New England summers. When he composed his little chronicle of the three weeks he spent with his son, he was not stealing time for other, more important projects. It was the only work he did, the only work he wanted to do.

The move to Lenox had been precipitated by Hawthorne's disastrous experiences in Salem in 1849. As he put it in a letter to his friend Horatio Bridge, he had come to dislike the town "so much that I hate to go into the streets, or to have the people see me. Anywhere else, I shall at once be entirely another man." Appointed to the post of surveyor in the Salem

Custom House in 1846 during the Democratic administration of James Polk, Hawthorne accomplished almost nothing as a writer during the three years he held this job. With the election of Whig candidate Zachary Taylor in 1848, Hawthorne was sacked when the new administration took office in March 1849 — but not without raising a great noise in his own defense, which led to a highly publicized controversy about the practice of political patronage in America. At the precise moment when this struggle was being waged, Hawthorne's mother died after a short illness. The notebook entries from those days in late July are among the most wrenching, emotionally charged paragraphs in all of Hawthorne. "Louisa pointed to a chair near the bed; but I was moved to kneel down close to my mother and take her hand. She knew me, but could only murmur a few indistinct words — among which I understood an injunction to take care of my sisters. Mrs. Dike left the chamber, and then I found the tears slowly gathering in my eyes. I tried to keep them down, but it would not be — I kept filling up, till, for a few moments, I shook with sobs. For a long time, I knelt there, holding her hand; and surely it is the darkest hour I ever lived."

Ten days after his mother's death, Hawthorne lost his fight to save his job. Within days of his dismissal (perhaps even the same day, if family legend is to be believed), he began writing *The Scarlet Letter*, which was completed in six months. Under great financial strain during this period his fortunes took a sudden, unexpected turn for the better just as plans were being made by the firm of Ticknor and Fields to publish the novel. By private, anonymous subscription, friends and supporters of Hawthorne (among them, most likely, Longfellow and Lowell) "who admire your genius and respect your character. . . [and to pay] the debt we owe you for what you have done for American literature" had raised the sum of five hundred dollars to help see Hawthorne through his difficulties. This windfall allowed Hawthorne to carry out his increasingly urgent desire to leave Salem, his hometown, and become "a citizen of somewhere else."

After a number of possibilities fell through (a farm in Manchester, New Hampshire, a house in Kittery, Maine), he and Sophia eventually settled on the red farmhouse in Lenox. It was, as Hawthorne put it to one of his former Custom House co-workers, "as red as the Scarlet Letter." Sophia was responsible for finding the place, which was situated on a larger property known as Highwood, currently being rented by the Tappan family. Mrs. Tappan, née Caroline Sturgis, was a friend of Sophia's, and it was she who offered the house to the Hawthornes — free of charge. Hawthorne, wary of the complications that might arise from living off the generosity of others, struck a bargain with Mr. Tappan to pay a nominal rent of seventy-five dollars for four years.

One would assume that he was satisfied with the arrangement, but that didn't stop him from grumbling about any number of petty annoyances. No sooner did the family settle into the house than Hawthorne came down with a bad cold, which confined him to bed for several days, and before long he was complaining in a letter to his sister Louisa that the farmhouse was "the most inconvenient and wretched little hovel that I ever put my head in." (Even the optimistic Sophia, who tended to see every adversity in the best possible light, admitted in a letter to her mother that it was "the smallest of ten-foot houses" — barely adequate for a family of four, let alone five.) If the house displeased Hawthorne, he had even harsher things to say about the landscape that surrounded it. Sixteen months after moving in, he wrote to his publisher, James T. Fields, "I have staid here too long and too constantly. To tell you a secret, I am sick to death of Berkshire, and hate to think of spending another winter here. . . . The air and climate do not agree with my health at all; and, for the first time since I was a boy, I have felt languid and dispirited, during almost my whole residence here. Oh that Providence would build me the merest little shanty, and mark me out a rood or two of garden-ground, near the sea-coast." Two years later, long after he had moved away and resettled in Concord, he was still grinding the same axe, as shown in this passage from the introduction to *Tanglewood Tales* (a second volume of Greek myths for children): "But, to me, there is a peculiar quiet charm in these broad meadows and gentle eminences. They are better than mountains, because they do not stamp and stereotype themselves into the brain, and thus grow wearisome with the same strong impression, repeated day after day. A few summer weeks among mountains, a lifetime among green meadows and placid slopes, with outlines forever new, because continually fading out of the memory. Such would be my sober choice." It is ironic that the area around Lenox should still be referred to as "Tanglewood." The word was Hawthorne's invention and is now indelibly associated with the music festival that takes place there every year. For a man who hated the area and ran away from it after just eighteen months, he left his mark on it forever.

Still, it was the best moment of his life, whether he knew it or not. Solvent, successfully married to an intelligent and famously devoted woman, in the middle of the most prolific writing burst of his career, Hawthorne planted his vegetable garden, fed his chickens, and played with his children in the afternoon. The shyest and most reclusive of men, known for his habit of hiding behind rocks and trees to avoid talking to people he knew, Hawthorne largely kept to himself during his stint in the Berkshires, avoiding the social activities of the local gentry and appearing in town only to collect his mail at the post office and return home. Solitude was his natural element, and considering the circumstances of his life until his early thirties, it was remarkable that he had married at all. When you were a person whose ship-captain father had died in Surinam when you were four, when you had grown up with a remote and elusive mother who had lived in a state of permanent, isolated widowhood, when you had served what is probably the most stringent literary apprenticeship on record — locking yourself up in your room for twelve years in a house you had dubbed "Castle Dismal" and leaving Salem only in the summer to go on solitary rambles through the New England countryside — then perhaps the society of your immediate family was sufficient. Hawthorne had married late to a woman who had likewise married late, and in the twenty-two years they lived together, they were rarely apart. He called her Phoebe, dove, Beloved, Dearissima, Ownest One. "Sometimes (for I had no wife then to keep my heart warm)," he had written to her during their courtship in 1840, "it seemed as if I were already in the grave, with only life enough to be chilled and benumbed. . . till at length a certain Dove was revealed to me, in the shadow of a seclusion as deep as my own had been. And I drew nearer and nearer to the Dove, and opened my bosom to her. . . keeping my heart warm, and renewing my life with her own. . . Thou only has taught me that I have a heart — thou only has thrown a light deep downward, and upward, into my soul. Thou only hast revealed me to myself; for without thy aid, my best knowledge of myself would have been merely to know my own shadow — to watch it flickering on the wall, and mistake its fantasies for my own real actions. . . Now, dearest, dost thou comprehend what thou has done for me?"

They lived in isolation, but visitors nevertheless came (relatives, old friends), and they were in contact with several of their neighbors. One of them, who lived six miles down the road in Pittsfield, was Herman Melville, then thirty-one years old. Much has been written about the relationship between the two writers (some of it pertinent, some of it nonsense), but it is clear that Hawthorne opened up to the younger Melville with unaccustomed enthusiasm and took great pleasure in his company. As he wrote to his friend Bridge on August 7, 1850: "I met Melville, the other day, and liked him so much that I have asked him to spend a few days with me before leaving these parts." Melville had only been visiting the area at the time, but by October he was back, acquiring the property in Pittsfield he renamed Arrowhead and installing himself in the Berkshires as a full-time resident. Over the next thirteen months, the two men talked, corresponded, and read each other's work, occasionally traveling the six miles between them to stay as a guest at the other's house. "Nothing pleases me more," Sophia wrote to her sister Elizabeth about the friendship between her husband and Melville (whom she playfully referred to as Mr. Omoo), "than to sit & hear this growing man dash his tumultuous waves of thought against Mr. Hawthorne's great, genial, comprehending silences. . . . Without doing anything on his own, except merely *being*, it is astonishing how people make him their innermost Father Confessor." For Melville, the encounter with Hawthorne and his writings marked a fundamental turn in his life. He had already begun his story about the white whale at the time of their first meeting (projected as a conventional high-seas adventure novel), but under Hawthorne's influence the book began to change and deepen and expand, transforming itself in an unabated frenzy of inspiration into the richest of all American novels, *Moby-Dick.* As everyone who has read the book knows, the first page reads: "In token of my admiration for his genius this book is inscribed to Nathaniel Hawthorne." Even if Hawthorne had accomplished nothing else during his stay in Lenox, he unwittingly served as Melville's muse.

Melville makes a couple of appearances in *Twenty Days with Julian & Little Bunny,* but the gist of the piece is the little boy himself, the daily activities of father and son, the ephemeral nothings of domestic life. No dramas are reported, the routine is fairly monotonous, and in terms of content, one can hardly imagine a duller or more pedestrian undertaking. Hawthorne kept the diary for Sophia. It was written in a separate family notebook which they both used to record material about the children (and which the children had access to as well, sometimes adding drawings and infant scribbles of their own — and, in a few instances, even tracing their pencils directly over texts written by their parents). Hawthorne intended his wife to read the little work after her return from West Newton, and it appears that she did so at the earliest opportunity. Describing the trip home to Lenox in a letter to her mother three days later (August 19, 1851), Sophia wrote, ". . . Una was very tired, and her eyes looked as cavernous as Daniel Webster's till she saw the red house; and then she began to shout, and clap her hands for joy. Mr. Hawthorne came forth with a thousand welcomes in his eyes, and Julian leaped like a fountain, and was impossible to hold fast. . . . I found that Mr. Hawthorne had written a minute account of his and Julian's life from the hour of our departure. . . ."

———

Why publish it now as an independent work? Why should this small uneventful piece of prose command our interest more than 150 years after it was written? I wish I could mount a cogent defense on its behalf, make some dazzling, sophisticated argument that would prove its greatness, but if the piece is great, it is great only in miniature, great only because the writing, in and of itself, gives pleasure. *Twenty Days* is a humorous work by a notoriously melancholic man, and anyone who has ever spent an extended length of time in the company of a small child will surely respond to the accuracy and honesty of Hawthorne's account.

———

All this lies behind the spirit of *Twenty Days with Julian & Little Bunny*. The Hawthornes were a consciously progressive family, and for the most part their treatment of their children corresponds to attitudes prevalent among the secular middle-class in America today. No harsh discipline, no physical punishment, no strident reprimands. Some people found the Hawthorne children obstreperous and unruly, but Sophia, ever inclined to see them as model creatures, happily reported in a letter to her mother that at a local torchlight festival "the children enjoyed themselves extremely, and behaved so beautifully that they won all hearts. They thought that there was never such a superb child as Julian, nor such a grace as Una. 'They are neither too shy, nor bold,' said Mrs. Field, 'but just right.'" What constitutes "just right," of course, is a matter of opinion. Hawthorne, who was always more rigorous in his observations than his wife — unable, by force of instinct and habit, to allow love to color his judgments — makes no bones about how annoying Julian's presence sometimes was to him. That theme is sounded on the first page of the diary, and it recurs repeatedly throughout the twenty days they spent together. The boy was a champion chatterbox, a pint-sized engine of logorrhea, and within hours of Sophia's departure, Hawthorne was already complaining that "it is impossible to write, read, think, or even to sleep (in the daytime) so constant are his appeals to me in one way or another." By the second evening, after remarking once again on the endless stream of babble that issued from Julian's lips, Hawthorne put him to bed and added: "Nor need I hesitate to say that I was glad to get rid of him — it being my first relief from his society during the whole day. This may be too much of a good thing." Five days later, on August 3, he was again harping on the same subject: "Either I have less patience today than ordinary, or the little man makes larger demands upon it; but

it really does seem as if he had baited me with more questions, references, and observations, than mortal father ought to be expected to endure." And again on August 5: "He continues to pester me with his inquisitions. For instance, just now, while he is whittling with my jack-knife. 'Father, if you had bought all the jack-knives in the shop, what would you do for another, when you broke them all?' 'I would go somewhere else,' say I. But there is no stumping him so. 'If you had bought all the jack-knives in the world, what would you do?' And here my patience gives way, and I entreat him not to trouble me with any more foolish questions. I really think it would do him good to spank him, apropos to this habit." And once again on August 10: "Mercy on me, was ever man before so be-pelted with a child's talk as I am!"

These little bursts of irritation are precisely what give the text its charm — and its truth. No sane person can endure the company of a high-voltage child without an occasional meltdown, and Hawthorne's admissions of less-than-perfect calm turn the diary into something more than just a personal album of summer memories. There is sweetness in the text, to be sure, but it is never cloying (too much wit, too much bite), and because Hawthorne refrains from glossing over his own faults and downcast moments, he takes us beyond a strictly private space into something

more universal, more human. Again and again, he curbs his temper whenever he is on the verge of losing it, and the talk of spanking the boy is no more than a passing impulse, a way of letting off steam with his pen instead of his hand. By and large, he shows remarkable forbearance in dealing with Julian, indulging the five-year-old in his whims and escapades and cockeyed discourses with steadfast equanimity, readily all-owing that "he is such a genial and good-humored little man that there is certainly an enjoyment intermixed with all the annoyance." In spite of the difficulties and possible frustrations, Hawthorne was determined not to rein in his son too tightly. After the birth of Rose in May, Julian had been forced to tiptoe around the house and speak in whispers. Now, suddenly, he is permitted to "shout and squeal just as loud as I please," and the father sympathizes with the boy's craving for commotion. "He enjoys this freedom so greatly," Hawthorne writes on the second day, "that I do not mean to restrain him, whatever noise he makes."

The diary includes many keenly written passages about the shifting light of the landscape (few novelists looked at nature as attentively as Hawthorne did) and a handful of droll and increasingly sympathetic descriptions of Hindlegs, the pet rabbit, who unfortunately expired as the chronicle was coming to an end. More and more, however, as his solitude dragged on, Hawthorne yearned for his wife to come home. By the beginning of the final week, that feeling had been turned into constant ache. After putting Julian to bed on the evening of August 10, he suddenly let himself go, breaking down in a rhapsodic gush of longing and allegiance. "Let me say outright, for once, that he is a sweet and lovely little boy, and worthy of all the love that I am capable of giving him. Thank God! God bless Phoebe for giving him to me! God bless her as the best wife and mother in the world! God bless Una, whom I long to see again! God bless Little Rosebud! God bless me, for Phoebe's and all their sakes! No other man has so good a wife, nobody has better children. Would I were worthier of her and them!" The entry then concludes: "My evenings are all dreary, alone, and without books that I am in the mood to read; and this evening was like the rest. So I went to bed about nine, and longed for Phoebe."

Nineteenth-Century Salem

By Wendell Garrett

Divitis Indiae, usque ad ultimum sinum
(To the farthest port of the rich East)
Motto on the seal of the city of Salem, Massachusetts

The creaking of timbers and the splash of the bow wave were the comforting sounds of a Salem ship in the East India trade bowling along before a following breeze. Salem's web of deep-water trade routes between 1790 and 1807 — the city's golden age — embraced the world: from Lima to Canton, from Saint Petersburg to Capetown, from Archangel to Trieste. For Salem's brash merchant-ship owners no port was too distant, no waters too dangerous, no risk too great. So common were her ships in Far Eastern ports that one wealthy trader there "believed Salem to be a country by itself, and one of the richest and most important sections of the globe."

Massachusetts, with its long coastline and abundance of good harbors, became a maritime commonwealth out of necessity, and its seamen and merchant adventurers tapped a vast reservoir of wealth and exotic imports from China and the East Indies. "Trade occupies all their thoughts, turns their heads, and absorbs all their speculations," wrote J. P. Brissot de Warville about Boston in 1788. Boston's most formidable rival in maritime commerce was Salem, which in 1790 was the sixth largest city in the United States with a little under eight thousand inhabitants. The sea traders of Salem had established a base at Isle de France (now Mauritius) from which their ships fanned out across the Indian Ocean to the Arabian Sea, Bay of Bengal, China Sea, and beyond to the South Pacific. The *Grand Turk* of Salem, under Captain Ebenezer West, was the first Massachusetts vessel to visit the Far East, and her return on May 22, 1787, brought fabulous profits to her owner. Her voyage challenged the ingenuity and energy of every Massachusetts mariner to sail "to the farthest port of the rich East," as Salem's municipal seal proclaims. In the race for Oriental opulence and luxury goods, "Boston was the Spain, Salem the Portugal," in the words of Samuel Eliot Morison.

For half a mile along Salem's harbor front runs Derby Street, with the long finger of Derby Wharf extending into the harbor in front of the Custom House, the residential and business center of the town in the eighteenth and nineteenth centuries. On one side were the brick and wooden mansions of the merchant-ship owners — the Derbys, Princes, Crowinshields and Peabodys. Opposite were wharves, warehouses, shipyards, ship chandlers, ropewalks and sail makers, all seen against a background of sails and spars and ships' rigging. With suitable oak and pine so close to the water's edge, the shipyards of Essex County had a long, proud tradition of building wonderful vessels for the Salem ship owners.

Virtually surrounded by water, Salem's appearance reflected its dependence on the sea. Sprawling shipyards and the dozens of wharves that extended the city into Salem Harbor dominated the waterfront. Commercial traffic in the harbor ranged from trans-Atlantic three-masted ships to schooners from Maine bringing firewood and timber for the ship-builders. Crowded wharves held the mounting goods: hogsheads of molasses, casks of rum, sacks of indigo, pipes of wine, stacks of lumber, bundles of hides, and barrels of sugar, salt, fish and beef. The established merchants of the "ancient and respectable families" still lived on Derby Street near their wharves and warehouses, but Essex Street was the increasingly fashionable site for large, richly furnished Federal style houses that John Adams called "the most elegant and grand I have seen in any of the maritime towns." To cut the costs of processing molasses and hides, merchants built their own distilleries and tanneries, the latter relegated

Salem center in the mid-nineteenth century. At the time the courthouse faced south on Washington Street.

to the area between the Common and Collins Cove because of the smell. The less affluent seamen and artisans lived on the lower ground near the waterfront. On the wharves, high and low mingled with foreign seamen and even an occasional visitor from the East. Salem was both a self-contained community of seafarers and a sophisticated center of world trade.

Sail reached its culmination in nineteenth-century naval and commercial vessels — a marriage of beauty and utility rarely matched by steam. In port cities like Salem, the pride of the community was embodied in the ships riding in its harbor. Many of Salem's citizens were involved in building, fitting and supplying them, and more than a few had interests in the vessels. The city regularly sent over a tenth of its citizens on dangerous sea voyages. Salem embraced the world. No port was too distant, no waters too dangerous. However, the ocean knows no favorites and a mariner's life was a precarious calling, as many of Salem's more than four hundred widows in 1783 would have testified. Sunken ledges and sandy shoals along New England's coast claimed many hapless vessels driven before a winter gale or lost in a thick summer fog. From the earliest times, during periods of international turmoil, many American merchantmen were sunk or captured on the high seas or confiscated in port.

At its peak in 1807, Salem was in full flower as a busy, prosperous, and cosmopolitan seaport of 10,000 inhabitants, most of whom made their living from the sea. And by that time, Salem's fleet numbered some 200 vessels. Some of the town's seafaring citizens knew cities like Bombay and Nagasaki better than Boston and New York. Salem had been a prosperous port for a century and a half before it ventured beyond the Cape of Good Hope, but its flowering came in the wake of vessels pioneering the Eastern routes and opening markets to American trade. The Indies trade put Salem on the world map, giving the town its style and character. It was a relatively small port, but one that held its own in world markets with the large merchantmen of the East India Company fleets.

More than any other port, Salem was identified with the Eastern luxuries trade. The freighting of necessities was at best a secondary business in Salem. The port's East Indiamen, called "floating bazaars," offered a variety of fine goods bought by the ship owner for speculation on world markets. Dozens of goods were handled, but there were trade staples on which the port's prosperity was founded. A Salem ship bound for the East left the wharf with West Indies molasses and sugar; European hardware, cheese and cloth; and American rum, cod, tobacco, barrel staves, butter, beef and ginseng. The Chinese believed ginseng — "the dose for immortality" — to be a panacea and aphrodisiac. It was one of the few western products that stirred their interest.

The waterside Yankees of New England were formidable profit-takers. They made money, and lost it, by buying, bartering, smuggling, shipping and selling whatever commodity turned a profit. They sold cod to the Roman Catholic countries, carried back the heavy wines of the Mediterranean littoral and Atlantic islands, and traded sandalwood, *bêche-de-mer*, birds' nests for soup, mother-of-pearl, and sea otter pelts in Canton. For their goods the captains obtained China tea, Arabian coffee, Sumatran pepper, and Indian sugar and cotton textiles. Supplementing these typical cargoes were cocoa, spices including cloves, cinnamon and ginger, ivory, wine, hides, gold dust and fine silks and porcelains from China. However, profits entail risks, and Yankee ships were sunk on coral reefs, lost in tropical storms, burned by disgruntled natives, seized by pirates, and destroyed by British and French men-of-war.

If these New England merchants were economically adventurous, they were politically and intellectually conservative. Emerson's comment that there "was not a book, a speech, a conversation, or a thought" in Massachusetts from 1790 to 1830 worth noticing was harsh, but not wholly inaccurate. Politically, their thinking was represented by the most skilled vituperator of the high Federalists, Fisher Ames, who believed that the new nation was "too big for union, too sordid for patriotism, and too democratic for liberty." In retirement old John Adams scorned the Boston merchant's preoccupation with making money. In a letter to his son, John Quincy Adams, he warned against diverting people "from the cultivation of the earth to adventures upon the sea," and accused Boston's merchants of "stiff-rumped stupidity." Nonetheless, the outbreak of war between England and France in 1793 gave these merchants their chance to reap soaring profits as neutral carriers between the warring parties. In their search for new markets and quick returns, New England shipmasters fanned out to ports around the Indian Ocean and in the Pacific on their way to Canton to engage in the China Trade.

The impact of the exotic imports from the Far East on Salem was palpable and startling. The Eastern luxuries trade became the special province of the port, gaining for it a reputation as the Venice of the New World. The people of Salem never grew jaded by the arrival of an East Indiaman from around the Cape of Good Hope. In the port's busiest years, when scores of sails brightened the harbor and the world's goods crowded its wharves, such a voyage underpinned Salem's prosperity and focused its spirit of community. The financial and physical risks taken by the merchants and crews made Salem by 1800 the nation's richest city per capita, with an air of sophistication and worldliness rivaling Boston. Fortunes accumulated in the East India trade maintained Samuel McIntire, Salem's master wood carver and presiding genius of Federal architecture. But Thomas Jefferson's embargo of December 22, 1807, and the War of 1812 undid Salem's fleet, which dwindled from 182 sail in 1807 to 57 in 1815.

No one in Salem was neutral about the embargo. When Jefferson shut down foreign trade in and out of United States ports, the action tore apart the once-solid merchant class, marking a turning point in Salem's fortunes. The embargo was supposed to force the combatants to recognize the rights of neutral traders by denying American goods to French and English markets. But the inclusion of the Indies and China trades in the ban crippled New England's commerce and undermined Salem's economy. Even firewood could not be brought in, and it was a cold, miserable winter. Staunch pro-British Federalists in Salem like the Derbys denounced republicanism and pressed for nullification; extremists among them seriously considered secession from the Union, and were called by their opposition the "Essex Junto" (from Essex County). The Republican Crowinshields supported Jefferson and the embargo, in spite of the stigma their stand brought on themselves, and Federalists labeled them "Jacobins" after the French revolutionary party.

Salem from Witches Hill

With its fleet cut to a fourth of its size before "Mr. Madison's War," Salem found recovery difficult. When peace came in 1815, the Federalists Party's near "traitorous" stance destroyed its national stature. And when commerce could resume on the global scale of the previous decade, American merchants found that critical changes had occurred and the increased English competition was now intense and successful. Newburyport and Salem on the North Shore and Plymouth to the south would never again have their commercial importance. Only the commercial eminence of Boston would be enhanced as a centralization of overseas trade developed in the 1820s and 1830s. The Reverend William Bentley (1759-1819) witnessed the port's decline during his own final years, lamenting in his diary about "the stagnation of Commerce." Commerce was giving way to infant industries, and after the High Federalist's unpopular stand against the recent war, they no longer had the influence to guarantee pro-shipping legislation in Washington. More and more Salem merchants turned from wharf to waterfall, investing in the burgeoning textile mills along the Merrimack River rather than sending their capital to distant markets after scarce commodities.

But despite the fading of Salem's glory, the town's slide was not so precipitous as in other small port towns. Because its trade was specialized, it was able to hold markets longer. Merchants changed their trade patterns, sending out vessels on shorter voyages, trading cargo for cargo and returning home. They sought out new markets: South America, the Maritime Provinces, the South Sea islands. Salem's final great commerce was on the east coast of Africa — the Zanzibar trade. The gum copal for making varnish brought from there in 1827 became the port's last trade monopoly.

When New York City gained the edge in the new western markets with the completion of the Erie Canal in 1825, Boston forestalled its own decline by developing its rail connections, drawing foreign trade away from Salem and Newburyport. The exodus of merchants to Boston and New York, following the profits, quickened and they grew discouraged by stiffening competition.

Even though the great dynasties dissolved, fortunes could still be made in Salem. Joseph Peabody was the wealthiest merchant-ship owner of Salem between the embargo and his death in 1844. In his lifetime he owned at least part interest in 63 vessels, sailed by 7,000 seamen. He made his fortune in the Sumatran pepper trade, and almost alone carried on the China, India and East Indies trades during Salem's declining years. His brig *Leander,* built at Salem in 1821, made twenty-six voyages to Europe, Asia Minor, Africa and the Far East in the twenty-three years of her life. His ship *George* made twenty-one round trip voyages from Salem to Calcutta between 1815 and 1837, with such regularity that she was called the "Salem Frigate." The *George* was a veritable training ship; no less than twenty-six mates and forty-five captains graduated from the forecastle of this floating bit of Essex County.

In the port's declining years, Joseph Peabody almost single-handedly carried on the Calcutta, the China and the Sumatra voyages. Although for another fifty years a dwindling number of Salem firms traded with the Far East, Salem ceased to be an important seaport in 1845. That was the year when President James K. Polk appointed Nathaniel Hawthorne surveyor of the port of Salem, where he dreamed away the idle days between the arrival of occasional ships. When he wrote *The Scarlet Letter* after losing his position upon the 1849 election of the Whigs, President Zachery Taylor dismissed him in an action that caused national press attention. In *The Custom House Introductory to The Scarlet Letter* Hawthorne drew a true and enduring picture of Salem's gentle decay in his description of the lazy, ancient bureaucrats lolling lazily back in their secure government jobs with little to do.

In 1848, with the establishment of the Naumkeag Steam Cotton Mills, built on the site of Briggs' shipyard, Salem entered the factory era; and a fluttering drone of spindles began to dominate the empty harbor and idle wharves. The Salem merchants turned their East Indiamen into "trucks," bringing in raw cotton, hides, gum copal, jute and wood, and distributing the manufactured textiles, shoes, varnish, burlap and woolens.

Salem's ocean-going sailing vessels established trade networks that for two centuries were the port's vital arteries. They were also the vanguard of America's economic and cultural expansion. While explorers on land to the West opened up the continent, maritime merchants, captains and their crews brought America into the world community. Salem's major role in opening the eastern trade is only one facet of the city's long and eventful maritime life. From its earliest days, when hungry colonists turned from New England's stony soil to the sea, through the era when virtually every citizen depended on shipping, to the last years when youths looked to Salem's cotton mills rather than its declining merchant fleet for work, the port's history is told through its changing relationship with the sea.

The Peabody Sisters of Salem

By Peggy Strong

The three Peabody sisters of Salem collectively personified and expressed a kaleidoscope of churning intellectual forces. They encountered and embraced the new ideas that were tugging restlessly at the coattails of traditional ideologies. Against this background of tension and change the sisters managed to hold on tightly to their belief in the value and power of education, and the need for social justice.

Nathaniel Peabody, the founding father of the famous Peabody clan, was descended from Francis Peabody, who had arrived in Salem in 1635. Nathaniel, a rather mild and absent-minded man, who had graduated from Dartmouth College in 1800 and taught Latin at Phillips Andover Academy, drifted into dentistry and moved his young family first to Cambridge, in order to attend medical lectures at Harvard, and then settled in Salem. His wife Elizabeth (Palmer) Peabody, whom he married in 1802, was the granddaughter of a famous Massachusetts Revolutionary general. Her sister was married to Royall Tyler, the Vermont jurist and first American playwright.

The family was thus well connected, if poorly financially supported. The mother taught school, and lent an imperative tone to the household, and the three daughters — the famous Peabody sisters of Salem —

responded to her decisive influence. They were raised in an atmosphere of financial hardship but, being well educated, the girls were imbued with the spirit of excellence, a strongly developed social conscience, and a sense of the importance of education. The three sisters, in addition, had personalities that attracted interesting and famous people. Their three brothers were younger and have since been forgotten. Elizabeth Palmer Peabody (1804-1894), the eldest, was to become famous as a social and educational reformer. She never married. The second daughter was Mary Peabody Mann (1806-1887), who shared in the work of her husband, the educator Horace Mann. The third daughter was Sophia Amelia Peabody (1809-1871), an artist and writer who married Nathaniel Hawthorne in one of American literature's most noted and supportive relationships. When her husband was absorbed in his work Sophia referred to him as her Hyperion, because of his shining look.

Elizabeth was born on May 16, 1804, in Billerica, Massachusetts. Her father, a school teacher at the time of his marriage, taught her Latin and inspired her eventual mastering of ten languages. Her mother, who conducted a school in Salem on the principle that every child should receive the training appropriate to genius, was the more decisive influence. Through her school and much private tutoring she developed in Elizabeth a precocious interest in theology, philosophy, history and literature. Her unusual approach to the education of the very young furnishes an important clue to Elizabeth's future involvement in educational reform.

It was Elizabeth Peabody's role as a teacher, Transcendentalist, author, and educational reformer, which made possible her early independence from her family and led to her acquaintance with William Ellery Channing, Bronson Alcott and other New England intellectuals. Her reading and speculation under Channing's guidance in the 1820s and 1830s paralleled that being done in more lonely fashion by Emerson, Alcott, and future Transcendentalists, with the result that almost inevitably she took her place with Margaret Fuller as the other female charter member of the Transcendentalist Club in 1837.

The relation with Channing was important in other ways. Discovering that his admirers required printed copies of his sermons, she became his copyist, readying for the printer between 1826 and 1842 some fifty of his sermons. Elizabeth also served as a sounding board for Channing's ideas, modifying with her questions and objections the scope and emphasis in many of his sermons. Meanwhile, her financial situation, always precarious, had worsened. Her school in the Boston suburb of Brookline had closed in 1832, and for a time she subsisted on a scant income pieced together from private tutoring, and from delivering lectures on various subjects, for which young matrons paid by subscription. During this period she became acquainted with the educator Horace Mann who lived in the same boardinghouse as the Peabody sisters. For a time a romantic attachment seemed about to develop between Mann and Elizabeth, but it was her sister Mary whom he eventually married.

In 1834 a new intellectual adventure began. Bronson Alcott had sensed the depth of Elizabeth Peabody's concern with education soon after their first meeting in 1830. When he arrived in Boston from Pennsylvania, she encouraged him to establish a school, then transferred to him the students she had gathered for a new school of her own, collected yet other children, and installed herself as his assistant. Elizabeth's *Record of a School* (1835), a journal in which she included her own comments, established Alcott as an important and contentious individual in avant-garde intellectual circles, and this role he himself expanded in 1836-1837 with his *Conversations with Children on the Gospels*, which contained further installments of Elizabeth's journal as well as other records by her sister Sophia Peabody Hawthorne.

These books brought Alcott under severe criticism for some remarks he made on pregnancy and childbirth in a discussion of Christ's Nativity. Elizabeth, by association, became a controversial figure and this had a disastrous effect on her career prospects. Severing her connection with Alcott's school in 1836, she returned to Salem, where for four years she lived with her family without income or employment. Here she discovered Nathaniel Hawthorne, whose family she had known since childhood, and who later, in 1842, became her sister Sophia's husband.

Two years before her youngest sister's marriage, Elizabeth moved her family from Salem to 13 West Street, Boston, where in the front parlor she opened one of the most influential and unusual bookstores in American history that soon became the headquarters of the Transcendentalists. Miss Peabody established herself as the first woman publisher in Boston and, it seems likely, in the nation. Her publications included a Channing pamphlet on Emancipation, three of Hawthorne's books for children, and, for a brief period, *The Dial,* a publication produced by Margaret Fuller and her Transcendentalist colleagues. In May 1849 appeared the single issue of Elizabeth's own Transcendentalist periodical, *Aesthetic Papers,* in which, with editorial boldness, she published Thoreau's "Civil Disobedience," destined to become a scripture for Ghandi and Martin Luther King.

Transcendentalism as an organized movement had ended by the mid-1840s, and she closed her bookshop around 1850, moving her ailing parents to West Newton, Massachusetts. After1850 the cause of Christian-Transcendental education for the young became the dominant passion of her life. She taught for a time and then, in 1859, went to live in Concord with her recently widowed sister Mary. From this point, most of Elizabeth's energy went into writing and lecturing on education: between 1850 and 1884 she produced ten books and fifty articles.

A pivotal year in her life was 1859 when, while teaching in an infant school in Concord, started by her sister Mary, she learned of the kindergarten movement founded in Germany by Friedrich Froebel. A year later, in Boston, she started the first formally organized kindergarten in the United States. The school attracted admiring attention, and Miss Peabody's *Moral Culture of Infancy, and Kindergarten Guide* (1863), written with Mrs. Mann, sold well. Elizabeth Palmer Peabody's most widespread impact on American life lay in her advocacy of the kindergarten movement. Her most significant achievement, however, was her contribution to American Transcendentalism, and appropriately she concluded her teaching career in the 1880's as a faculty member of Bronson Alcott's Concord School of Philosophy.

Vigorous to the end, she was unfailingly generous in her enthusiasms, and she has passed to posterity largely through the reminiscences of those who knew her in extreme old age. These reports reveal her as a colorful eccentric with an infectious passion for education and social justice. She died at her home in Jamaica Plain, Boston, on January 3, 1894 in her ninetieth year. The Elizabeth Peabody House, a Boston social settlement, was established in 1896 in her memory. Elizabeth's achievement lies not so much in her own intellectual gifts, though these were considerable, as in her ability to appreciate original thinking in others, draw it forth, publicize it, and transmit it. The range and stature of the men whose work she championed is impressive. In educational reform she forms a link between isolated visionaries, like her own mother, and the organized kindergarten movement of the later nineteenth century.

Mary Tyler Peabody Mann, the second of the children, was born in Cambridge, Massachusetts, on November 16, 1806, and married Horace Mann on May 1, 1843. Although she had little formal schooling, she grew up "in an atmosphere of education," as she later recalled, being surrounded by good books and intellectually stimulating people. At eighteen she left home to teach in Hallowell, Maine; the next year she moved to Boston, where she supported herself by helping her older sister, Elizabeth, conduct a "dame school" for young children in Brookline, which soon attracted a stream of tuition-paying pupils.

In 1832, while the two sisters were living in a Boston boardinghouse, they met Horace Mann, a fellow lodger and at that time a lawyer and state legislator. His wife had recently died, and to the Peabody sisters the handsome widower appeared clearly grief-stricken and distraught; both women offered him sympathy and tenderness, through which he gradually regained an interest in his work, but it was the more dominant Elizabeth who first became his special confidante. This intimacy, which she adamantly insisted was purely sisterly, heightened during the years between 1833-1835 while Mary, having taken her semi-invalid sister Sophia to the West Indies to recover her health, worked as a governess in a wealthy Cuban family. Probably both Mary and Elizabeth hoped to marry Mann, but he never considered the older sister as a wife and only gradually came to think of Mary, with her quiet feminine charm, as something more than a devoted and affectionate friend. For eight years after her return from Cuba, Mary toiled away at a succession of teaching posts, mostly in Salem. After the family moved to Boston in 1839 she provided increasing assistance to Mann during the early years of his educational reforms, copying numerous letters, and recording school reports and statistics which formed the basis for some of his famous *Annual Reports* as secretary of the new state board of education.

After they were married in 1843, the Manns settled in Boston, moving after a few years to West Newton. Mary supervised the rearing of their three children, providing a comfortable home for them and for her indefatigable husband. When Mann, having resigned his educational post in order to accept a seat in Congress, became embroiled in the antislavery movement, Mary, with her strong humanitarian sympathies, offered him constant support. In 1853 Mann accepted the presidency of Antioch College, a new nonsectarian coeducational school at Yellow Springs, Ohio. Mary Mann moved her family west with considerable optimism. The following years, however, were disappointing. The financial basis of the school was tenuous; the Manns were plagued by petty sectarian disputes, and Mary found the atmosphere of the small country town monotonous. In spite of all the disasters and setbacks, Mrs. Mann fulfilled her role as the president's wife and unofficial dean of women. Laboring against heavy odds, she coached the girls, all products of a rustic background and lifestyle, in the social graces and proprieties indigenous to better New England families.

After her husband's death in 1859 Mrs. Mann moved the family back to Concord, Massachusetts, where, resuming her old profession, she opened a school. In 1866 she bought a house in Cambridge so that her sons could attend Harvard. Meanwhile she had become closely associated with her sister Elizabeth's work with the kindergarten movement in Boston, handling much of the literary side of publicizing the new program while her sister traveled and lectured. Together they published *Moral Culture of Infancy, and Kindergarten Guide* (1863), in which she stressed the importance of a caring environment in the teaching of young children, and declared that the process of education should be one of eliciting and nurturing certain "faculties" within the child, rather than implanting facts by means of rote recitation.

Throughout her life Mary exhibited a remarkable degree of self-abnegation, accepting a supporting role to her famous husband and sister. Her literary accomplishments included her *Life and Works of Horace Mann*, published in three volumes (1865-1868). She also published *Christianity in the Kitchen: a Physiological Cookbook* (1857), a collection of recipes, common-sense health rules and admonitions against intemperance. At eighty she found time to write a novel, *Juanita: A Romance of Real Life in Cuba Fifty Years Ago* (1887). She died in Boston the following year on February 11, 1887, and was buried in Providence, Rhode Island, beside her husband and his first wife.

Sophia Amelia Peabody Hawthorne, the third daughter of the Peabodys, was born on September 21, 1809, in Salem, Massachusetts, later to become the wife of Nathaniel Hawthorne in 1842. She had little formal schooling, except that which she received at the age of eleven while

Sophia Amelia Peabody Hawthorne

attending classes held by her sister Elizabeth, then sixteen. However, Sophia was an avid reader, and she gained some competency in French, German, Latin, Greek, Hebrew, and possibly Italian. One of the distinguishing features, which set her apart from her two sisters, was her talent as an artist. In 1824 she began to study drawing. While never lazy, she was never well, and at fifteen she began to suffer from migraine headaches and to experience dreadful nightmares. She became reclusive, nervous and depressed. At this low point in her life, Hawthorne's appearance acted like sunshine in winter. She emerged from the dark secluded isolation of her room into the light of his presence.

During the 1830s she shared a studio with her friend Mary Newhall, where she painted, and sometimes sold, copies of other artist's work as well as her own original compositions. Her friends included not only the intellectuals who frequented the West Street family bookshop, briefly established in Boston, but artists like Washington Allston, who visited her studio to offer her criticism as well as encouragement. The artists George Flagg, G. P. A. Healy, Chester Harding and Thomas Doughty, were also her friends and teachers. Sophia was a diligent professional artist. Her illustration of Bronson Alcott talking with children at his school appeared as the frontispiece for the second volume of his *Conversations with Children on the Gospels* (1837), and she produced a considerable number of illustrations for the 1842 edition of Hawthorne's *Grandfather's Chair*. Perhaps her best known illustration is her frontispiece to the special edition of her husband's tale *The Gentle Boy*, the story of a child whose life is torn apart by the fiercely conflicting religious doctrines which divided Puritan from Quaker. Hawthorne dedicated the story to Sophia, and published it in 1839 as a gesture of his admiration and affection for the woman whom he later chose to be his wife. By the time of their marriage her skill as an artist was reflected in a number of Hawthorne's tales, and it was later to send them to Italy and to bring to life the fictional portrait of Hilda in *The Marble Faun.*

After a long and secret engagement beginning in 1838, Sophia Peabody and Nathaniel Hawthorne were married in the back parlor of the West Street house, in Boston, on July 9, 1842. After a simple ceremony, she and Nathaniel drove to their first home, the "Old Manse" in Concord, where they lived for the next four years. Their happiness there was recorded in several of Hawthorne's essays and in the journal which they jointly kept. Sophia had a natural eye for space, color and form. She knew instinctively where to place objects so that they appeared to the best advantage. She converted the dining room into her studio and, never doubting his literary genius, she organized a study upstairs where her husband could write. Using her diamond ring, Sophia and her husband scratched inscriptions on one of the window panes in this room which still survive and read: "Man's accidents are God's purposes / Sophia A. Hawthorne 1843"; "Nathl Hawthorne / This is his study / 1843"; and "The smallest twig / Leans clear against the sky. / Composed by my wife, / and written with her dia- / mond / Inscribed by my / husband at sunset / April 3d 1843 / On the gold light – SAH / Sund." Just as the fictional character of Phoebe, in *The House of the Seven Gables*, brought pleasure, happiness and order to the Pyncheon household, the real-life Sophia introduced those same qualities into the life of her husband and friends. The Hawthornes had three children: Una (born in 1844); Julian (1846), who became a minor novelist; and Rose (1851), who became a poet and the author of a memoir of her parents.

From 1850 to1851 Sophia and Nathaniel lived in Lenox, and for some months in 1851 they were at Horace Mann's home in West Newton, while Mann served in Congress. In 1852 they bought the Wayside, in Concord, next door to the Alcotts and down the road from the Emersons. This address served as their *pied-à-terre* for the rest of Hawthorne's life, though they were in Europe from 1853 to 1860, some of that time being spent in Liverpool, where Hawthorne served as American Consul. When they arrived in the thriving English seaport, Sophia was still only forty-four years old, and she loved the new life of fashionable parties attended by richly elegant and amusing new acquaintances. In 1860, while living in Italy, her husband conceived of *The Marble Faun*, a romance of

American artists living in Europe. The manuscript of *The Marble Faun* indicates that Sophia made significant changes to the text, even altering the name of one of the characters. Nathaniel's respect for his wife's literary talent is clearly expressed in words written to his Boston publisher, William D. Ticknor in 1857: "Her descriptions are the most perfect pictures that ever were put on paper." Her style of writing in her *Notes in England and Italy*, published by her cousin George Putnam, in 1869, are colorful and full of detail, her descriptions graphic and highly charged.

The years after the family's return to America were troubled ones. Una never recovered her health after the bout of malaria she suffered in Italy. Hawthorne's own health was poor. He became lethargic, and by 1863 writing was becoming a chore. He avoided society, and with the loss of his ability to write, he feared that he was losing his mind. Plagued by physical pain and periods of emotional agony, he eventually died in a hotel room in Plymouth, New Hampshire, in May 1864, the day before their daughter Rose's thirteenth birthday. A part of Sophia died with the man whom she loved and revered, the man who personified the wellspring of her strength and happiness, and from then on, the burden of supporting the family fell entirely on her own shoulders.

In the autumn of 1866 Julian was sent down from Harvard and Nathaniel's publisher, James T. Fields, announced that the investments he had made on their behalf had lost money. Sophia was actually in debt. On the advice of friends, she began editing her husband's notebooks. Sophia's substituted refinements, suppression of actual names and general softening of the text have drawn modern criticism, but in fact she followed the editorial fashion of her day. In 1868, in an impecunious state, Mrs. Hawthorne moved to Dresden, Germany, where she stayed until the summer of 1869. She then moved together with Rose and Una into a small terraced house in London, where the cold damp English weather disagreed with her. She became frail and eventually dangerously ill, having contracted typhoid pneumonia. Sophia, the youngest, most beautiful, and artistic of the sisters, was only sixty-one when she died on February 26, 1871. She is buried in Kensal Green cemetery, in London.

All three women were writers, and all three moved freely in the high Victorian and male-dominated world of intellectual exploration and moral philosophy. Elizabeth, Mary and Sophia demonstrated, in their own inimitable ways, a tireless and selfless effort for the good of others.

The Old Manse by Ross Turner

The location pleased Hawthorne's sense of privacy because its site was not "so imminent upon the road that every passer-by can thrust his head, as it were, into the domestic circle" of the honeymooning couple. The Trustees of Reservations maintains the Concord house today.

Henry David Thoreau, Hawthorne's Concord Gardener

By Laura L. Butters

My garden, that skirted the avenue of the Manse, was of precisely the right extent . . . I used to visit and revisit it a dozen times a day, and stand in deep contemplation over my vegetable progeny with a love that nobody could share or conceive of who had never taken part in the process of creation.

— *Mosses from an Old Manse*: The Old Manse

On July 9, 1842, in the early afternoon with sunlight streaming in, Nathaniel Hawthorne and Sophia Peabody were married in the parlor of her family's home (and the site of her sister Elizabeth's bookshop) on West Street in Boston. After the simple ceremony, they journeyed by carriage to Concord and took up residence at The Old Manse, on the banks of the Concord River.

An arrangement had been made with the current owner, Samuel Ripley (uncle of Ralph Waldo Emerson), for rental of the property, complete with furnished house, for $100 per year. As the Hawthornes came up the drive "between two tall gateposts of roughhewn stone" they caught their first glimpse of the vegetable garden in the left field. Evidence shows that Cynthia Thoreau and/or Elizabeth Hoar requested Henry Thoreau to plant this vegetable garden as a wedding and welcome gift for the newlyweds.

Henry Thoreau does not make mention of this garden in his journals, but Nathaniel Hawthorne's journal entries are quite extensive on the subject. He gives a wonderful description of the cycles of the garden as well as what was grown in it. Hawthorne took on the care of the garden and watched over his "vegetable progeny" with the eye of an artist as well as a proud parent:

> *They* [summer squashes] *presented an endless diversity of urns and vases, shallow or deep, scalloped or plain, moulded in patterns which a sculptor would do well to copy, since Art has never invented any thing more graceful. A hundred squashes in the garden were worthy, in my eyes at least, of being rendered indestructible in marble.*
>
> Mosses From an Old Manse: The Old Manse

These works of art from Mother Nature graced the Hawthorne's table:

> *After breakfast, I go forth into my garden, and gather whatever the beautiful Mother has made fit for our present sustenance; and, of late days, she generally gives me two squashes and a cucumber, and promises me green corn and shell beans, very soon.*
>
> Journal, Saturday, August 13, [1842]

Of course, as all gardeners know, there is much toil required to produce these artful squashes:

> *I am forced, however, to carry on a continual warfare with the squash-bugs, who, were I to let them alone for a whole day together, would perhaps quite destroy the prospects of the whole summer. It is impossible not to feel bitterly angry with these unconscionable vermin, who scruple not to do such infinite mischief to me, with only the profit of a meal or two to themselves. . . There is an absolute pleasure in taking vengence on them.*
>
> Journal, Friday, June 23d, [1843]

Hawthorne and Henry Thoreau did strike up a friendship, and by August 5 of 1842, Thoreau had already been over and "twice listened to the music of the spheres, which, for our private convenience, we had packed into a musical box." The music box was one of the wedding gifts that the Hawthornes brought with them. It was not until September 1 that Hawthorne composed what is probably one of the better-known descriptions of Thoreau:

> *Mr. Thorow(sic) dined with us yesterday. He is a singular character — a young man with much of wild original nature still remaining in him. . . He is ugly as sin, long-nosed, queer-mouthed, and with uncouth and somewhat rustic, although courteous manners, corresponding very well with such an exterior. But his ugliness is of an honest and agreeable fashion, and becomes him much better than beauty.*
>
> Journal, Thursday, September 1st, [1842]

He continued on to say that Thoreau was a "keen and delicate observer of nature" and that "Nature, in return for his love, seems to adopt him as her especial child." He also maintained that Thoreau had a good knowledge of literature, poetry and "great regard for the memory of the Indian tribes."

That evening, after dinner, the two men journeyed on the Concord River in Thoreau's boat, Musketaquid. By the end of their journey, Hawthorne had agreed to buy the boat from him for seven dollars. This was the vessel that Thoreau and his brother John had built and sailed on the Concord and Merrimack Rivers.

The next day, Thoreau delivered the Musketaquid to The Old Manse and gave Hawthorne his first "lesson in rowing and paddling." Apparently, he was not as adept as Thoreau and "the boat seemed bewitched, and turned its head to every point of the compass except the right one." Thoreau then took the paddle and "the Musketaquid immediately became docile as a trained steed" and Hawthorne suspected "that she has not yet transferred her affections from her old master to her new one." He and Sophia then proposed to change the boat's name to Pond Lily — "which will be very beautiful and appropriate, as, during the summer season, she will bring home many a cargo of pond lilies from along the river's weedy shore."

In April of 1843, Thoreau stopped at The Manse to inform Hawthorne of his plans to "reside at Staten Island, as private tutor in the family of

Mr. [R.W.] Emerson's brother [William]." They discussed the spiritual advantages of a change of place, the *Dial* and Mr. [Bronson] Alcott. Hawthorne felt the change would be good for his friend, as lately, he had seemed out of sorts physically, mentally and morally. He preferred Thoreau to stay in Concord as he was one of the few persons "with whom to hold intercourse is like hearing the wind among the boughs of a forest-tree; and with all this wild freedom, there is high and classic cultivation . . . too."

Thoreau, remembering how much the Hawthorne's enjoyed their music box, asked them to keep his own music box while he was away. Thoreau's music box had been a gift from Margaret Fuller's younger brother whom he had tutored for advance admission to Harvard. Hawthorne listened to it over and over again to raise his spirits while Sophia was away visiting her sister Mary. However, he found eventually that "its peculiar sweetness has evaporated. . . It has not an infinite soul." Hawthorne found working in the garden to be a better occupation of his time.

As part of the Landscape Management Plan for The Old Manse, the re-introduction of a nineteenth century vegetable garden had always been intended. The varieties grown were to be determined by

information from Hawthorne's journals and George Bradford's (Samuel Ripley's brother-in-law) garden journal of Concord, in which he recorded all his gardening efforts at The Old Manse in the mid-to-late nineteenth century. The garden space measured approximately one-half acre and had been lying fallow since the 1920s. The Old Manse itself was built circa 1770 for Reverend William Emerson, grandfather of Ralph Waldo Emerson. The original 22-acre property was a working farm with kitchen garden and William Emerson was even the first person in Concord to cultivate potatoes. The Emerson-Ripley family owned the property until 1939, at which point they sold the remaining nine acres and furnished house to The Trustees of Reservations.

In 1996, The Old Manse joined forces with Gaining Ground, Inc. to reproduce this vegetable garden that had played such an important role in the Hawthornes' lives. Gaining Ground is a nonprofit organization whose mission is to grow and distribute fresh, organic produce to Boston-area meal programs, shelters and food pantries with the help of volunteers. They were founded in 1993 on privately-owned land and have since moved to a nine-acre plot behind the Henry Thoreau Birthplace on Virginia Road in Concord and the one-half acre heirloom garden at The Old Manse. The main problem for The Manse had been lack of time and staff to maintain such a project. Meanwhile, Gaining Ground was looking to expand their amount of cultivated land and, it also happened, that their garden coordinator was extremely interested in working with heirloom seed varieties. Most importantly, Gaining Ground's mission fit right in with The Trustees of Reservations mission to "preserve, for public use and enjoyment, properties of exceptional scenic, historic, and ecological value in Massachusetts." Ground was broken in April of 1997.

The garden was an immediate success on many levels: The Old Manse landscape was infused with a new level of visibility. Everyone, visitors and locals alike, wanted to know what was being grown and what the history of the garden was; groups of garden volunteers were being educated about The Old Manse as well as the gardening process; Gaining Ground had more land to work with; their garden coordinator was able to work with a local school whose students and staff grew tomatoes from seed, planted the seedlings and then returned in the fall to help clear the garden; collaborative public programs were created; and, in that first season, 5,000 pounds of produce were harvested and donated.

Since 1997, 24,000 pounds of produce have been harvested from this nineteenth-century heirloom garden at The Old Manse. The first year, the tomato plants were seven feet tall and produced fruit weighing five pounds. They are no longer that big or tall, but the garden continues to produce approximately 3,000 pounds a year. The vegetables and varieties are rotated from year to year and the plan is to eventually have a self-sustaining garden. In other words, the seeds are saved each year to be planted the next year or traded through groups like Seed-Savers or other heirloom seed exchanges.

Problems suffered by Hawthorne in 1842-45 with the garden continue today. With him it was squash bugs, and today's ongoing battle is with the potato beetle. The younger volunteers are usually given the job of "squishing them," as they say. Weeds are also a factor and Hawthorne's observations still hold true today:

> Why is it, I wonder, that Nature has provided such a host of enemies for every useful esculent, while the weeds are suffered to grow unmolested, and are provided with such tenacity of life, and such methods of propagation, that the gardener must maintain a continual struggle, or they will hopelessly overwhelm him!
>
> Journal, Friday, June 23d, [1843]

Nathaniel Hawthorne and Henry Thoreau would both be pleased to see the garden at The Old Manse continuing to provide for people today in both a practical and spiritual way.

> ... I felt that by my agency, something worth living for had been done. A new substance was born into the world. They were real and tangible existences, which the mind could seize hold of and rejoice in.
>
> Mosses From an Old Manse: The Old Manse

WORKS CITED:

Bradford, George. *Garden Journal of Concord.*
Private Collection, Concord Free Public Library

Hawthorne, Nathaniel. *Mosses From an Old Manse: The Old Manse.*
Centenary Edition, Ohio State University Press, 1974.

Hawthorne, Nathaniel. *The American Notebooks.* Ed. Claude M. Simpson
Centenary Edition, Ohio State University Press, 1972.

Mellow, James R. *Nathaniel Hawthorne in His Times.*
Boston: Houghton Mifflin Company, 1980.

The Novel and
The House of the
Seven Gables

By Alexandria Mason

"I think of such titles as — 'The House of the Seven Gables' there being that number of gable ends to the old shanty ...."[1] With these words from a letter to his editor regarding his newest work, Nathaniel Hawthorne not only entitled his third novel, but also set in motion a relationship that would change the destiny of an ancient structure and touch the lives of over 120,000 people annually. Did an actual house inspire the backdrop for Hawthorne's dark exploration of familial guilt? What was the relationship between a majestic mansion built by John Turner in 1668 in the town of Salem, Massachusetts, and the novel, *The House of the Seven Gables*? And how has the novel that Hawthorne wrote affected the Turner mansion?

The house's history is a long and vibrant one that began in 1668 when the young John Turner built his seaside mansion in expectation of his rapidly soaring social status. Newly married and already a successful mariner, John Turner quickly made the transition into what was then considered the elite social status of merchant and became active in the service of the crown. In addition to military actions, John Turner also served as selectman. It is interesting to note that Hawthorne's famous ancestor, the hanging judge of the Salem Witch Trails, John Hathorne, attended the meetings of the selectmen in Turner's Great Room. By his death, Turner was one of the wealthiest men in Essex County, and his house, which had grown as his wealth had, reflected his lofty status by the display of the finest examples of English Jacobean architectural elements. The second John Turner followed his father's lead, both in commerce and military roles. John Turner II was a larger-than-life swash-buckling figure who gained the title of colonel and assisted in the capture of the murderous pirate, Captain John Quelch. Sadly, the third John Turner fell upon hard times, and was forced to sell the family manse to Samuel Ingersoll in 1782, who provided the connection to Nathaniel Hawthorne through his only surviving heir, Susanna Ingersoll.

Samuel's daughter appears to have been a key figure from which Hawthorne drew inspiration for *The House of the Seven Gables*. Parallels with the household of Susanna Ingersoll, Hawthorne's cousin, can easily be drawn from both plot as well as the setting of the novel. Susanna, who never married, lived in the old Turner-Ingersoll mansion and, after the death of her parents, was faced with providing her own income. Without a husband or father to provide for her, this enterprising woman did what few women of her day dared — she created a profitable living through savvy real estate deals. We find in Salem records over a dozen transactions in which Miss Ingersoll bought, sold or mortgaged real estate. There is also documentation that this feisty lady pursued unpaid debt and ensured the proper payment of money she was due.

Her life as inspiration in the story seems clear enough when we read about Hepzibah, also a single, aging woman living in a great house alone, forced to provide an income for herself while beset by her unrelenting relatives. Salem diarist, the Reverend William Bentley, recounts a tale about young Susanna Ingersoll, at her mother Susanna's death, which could be a template for Hepzibah's plight in the novel:

> *The death of Madame Susanna Ingersoll. . . This morning I was*
> *with her only daughter who has been beset by the Col's family with*
> *the ferocity of tigers. They insisted upon entrance into the house &*
> *apartments. The daughter had swooned upon the death of her mother*
> *& was very low. I took such charge as she desired me for which I expect*

their vengeance. No prohibition could keep them out of the house. We talk of savages. What are we without our Laws & penalties... I first hid the money & then the keys. So much for hungry expectants & for having the intended heirs debtors. It was a curious scene to me. The daughter sick, as she says, in her prison. [2]

It would be some thirty years after this ugly scene that Hawthorne would visit his spinster cousin in the old Turner-Ingersoll mansion. It is tempting to imagine his shock and outrage when he learned of this event as the elderly woman, still indignant and wounded by the cruelty of her relations, recounted it to him. It too closely resembles the confrontation between Judge Jaffery Pyncheon and poor old Hepzibah to be discounted. If Susanna herself were to serve as a model for Hawthorne, it seems fitting enough then, too, that "her prison," which by the 1840s had already been witness to over one hundred and seventy years of Salem history, should play a major part.

Photos from the nineteenth century show the house in a very different form than today. In the 1790s, the fashion of multi-gables was quite passé and the square Federal form was at its height. As appropriate for a prosperous Salem sea captain, Susanna's father had updated the house to match the current fashion. In 1794, he had the rambling gabled back section removed and the overhanging second story boxed in to further perfect the desired sleek square that is the hallmark of Federal taste.[3] The chimneys had been rebuilt at some later point and were of a diminutive proportion, and, in all general aspects, the house was smaller and commanded much less awe than it had in bygone days.

This description does not conjure to mind the house in Hawthorne's tale. Indeed, when Henry James made his pilgrimage to the site in 1904 to behold the house that had served as a muse for Hawthorne, his reaction was less than enthusiastic. In speaking of his disappointment that Salem's ancient houses had bland visages that belied their deep, dark secrets, he noted they are poor witnesses, " ... as I was presently to learn, to my cost, from the dreadful anti-climax of the Seven Gables. They look brief and provisional at best — look, above all, incorrigible and witlessly innocent."[4] He decided not to enter the house, despite a placard inviting him to do so. [5] Had Henry James but stepped inside the deceptive facade, he might have had a better understanding of Hawthorne's inspiration.

One need only enter into the attic space for a moment to be transported in time to the earliest days of Colonial America. The attic has been a refuge from fleeting fashion and passing whim, and so it is almost a time capsule from the late 1600s. Despite restoration in 1910, the attic space retains much of what Hawthorne would have seen there. The sharply peaked roof is studded with nails which secured the original wooden shingles and their rust, combined with water stains, has created a weathered appearance that speaks of great age. At one gabled end the ancient nogging, or brick in-fill, and horsehair plaster are visible between the timbers of the house and call to mind the Elizabethan homes of England. The immense pine floorboards, which measure almost two feet wide, are uneven with wear. As one runs a hand along them, one feels the rise of the knots, which are more durable, and realizes that centuries of use by countless people have worn away the softer wood. Some of the 1668 timbers are still cloaked in their "waney edge," or bark clad exterior, and lend the space a primitive feel. Perhaps, however, the most riveting aspect is the scar of an original gable that was covered with the circa 1693 ell. This is where our view and Hawthorne's diverges and we must guess at what he witnessed before the 1910 restoration by Caroline O. Emmerton.

In some ways, the motivation for this restoration can be laid at Hawthorne's feet. Due to the popularity of the novel, *The House of the Seven Gables*, Miss Emmerton was moved to save the ancient house that had inspired the famous author by its romantic link to the past. She had a dual motivation to do so. Miss Emmerton, a philanthropic Salem citizen whose life was devoted to helping others, used the money generated by visitation to The House of the Seven Gables to fund her Settlement House. The Settlement House Movement at the turn of the last century gave newly arrived immigrants a helping hand in learning English, acquiring job skills and learning domestics trades. A multi-tasking and clever businesswoman, Caroline Emmerton capitalized on the popularity of Hawthorne's novel to fuel social services while preserving a structure she felt was important to posterity.

Through this, we may charge Mr. Hawthorne with exacting great influence on The House of the Seven Gables' destiny. Had he not created the novel which, at the local level, served as a monument to the house, it would have surely followed the fate of its many contemporaries and been destroyed in the name of modernization and progress. In addition to the

The House of the Seven Gables

great mansion, Miss Emmerton saved other historic Salem houses by moving them to her site and situating them in the shadow of great 1668 mansion. Foremost among these was the very house where Nathaniel Hawthorne was born in 1804. She moved it from its original location on Union Street and nestled it close to The House of the Seven Gables. Other important examples of early American architecture that she saved by moving to the site are the 1655 Retire Beckett House, the 1685 Hooper Hathaway house and an 1820s Counting House.

While we may thank Mr. Hawthorne for the fascination his novel created for The House of the Seven Gables, we must also realize it motivated fundamental physical change to the house. As mentioned above, by Hawthorne's time, the house had been stripped of several of its gables, and while the scars in the attic told him the story of their existence, there were only three gables ends visible from the exterior. Since Hawthorne had created a literary monument to the structure, Caroline Emmerton felt compelled to present that interpretation to the public. To this end, she set about with her architect, Joseph E. Chandler, to create the very house of the novel, and recorded the project in her book, *The Chronicles of Three Old Houses*.[6] Despite the existence of very specific seventeenth- and eighteenth-century room inventories that designate the rooms of the historic house by use, such as hall or parlor chamber, Miss Emmerton chose to ally the rooms to characters in the novel. And so, upon visiting in 1925, one would be shown into Phoebe's room, Clifford's room, or could browse through Hepzibah's shop.

While she did not go so far as to decorate the exterior with "...quaint figures, conceived in the grotesqueness of a Gothic fancy...," she did order a great clustered chimney like that described by Hawthorne.[7] Her architect carefully chose antique brick and laid them in a less-than-plumb manner that gave the impression they had been shifting and settling for many years. Based on the physical evidence in the house as well as Hawthorne's description, Miss Emmerton restored the house to reflect Hawthorne's vision:

> Halfway down a bystreet of one of our New England towns stands a rusty wooden house, with seven acutely peaked gables, facing towards various points of the compass, and a huge, clustered chimney in the midst. The street is Pyncheon Street; the house is the old Pyncheon house... The aspect of the venerable mansion has always affected me like a human countenance, bearing the traces not merely of outward storm and sunshine, but expressive, also, of the long lapse of mortal life, and accompanying vicissitudes that have passed within.[8]

Perhaps the most apparent influence on the physical changes of the house was Hawthorne's description of Hepzibah's cent shop. Analysis on the exact configuration of this space before the 1910 restoration is currently underway, but Caroline Emmerton followed Hawthorne's description to the letter. She made sure that, "In the front gable, under the impending brow of the second story, and contiguous to the street, was a shop door, divided horizontally in the midst, and with a window for its upper segment, such as is often seen in dwellings of a somewhat ancient date." [9] Many of the goods Hawthorne described in Hepzibah's shop can be found in this recreation, and to complete the feel of the novel's Cent Shop, Emmerton added a charming little bell over the door intended to chime upon the approach of a visitor.

Finally, due to the energetic enthusiasm surrounding Hawthorne's novel, the building now known as The House of the Seven Gables is host to over 120,000 visitors a year. This number is much greater than the visitation most other literary sites enjoy. While an exciting testimony to the continued popularity of both Hawthorne's novel and the house that bears its name, this visitation presents challenging issues in terms of preservation and proper stewardship of the ancient structure. This institution is dedicated to preserving Hawthorne's Birthplace and The House of the Seven Gables so that generations to come may enjoy a tactile connection to this great author.

So while there are many changes that Emmerton implemented to create a better setting for her novel-hungry audience, we must remember the qualification that Hawthorne himself made to his reader in the introduction of his novel. He stated that although some aspects of the story may be recognized as true historical experiences, he set his imagination free on flights of fancy. Perhaps, therefore, we should not tie ourselves solely to the chronological history of the structure, but celebrate that sense of venerable history, inspirational characters and solid permanence that is the very essence of this great house. The House of the Seven Gables, whose name is known the world over, softens the boundaries between past and present and allows us to slip unnoticed into historical tableaux. This exquisite relic is, in many ways, a reflection of Hawthorne's melding of time and space. Hawthorne's description of his novel also applies to the physical fabric of this mansion that allows us to "attempt to connect a bygone time with the very present that is flitting away from us. It is a legend prolonging itself, from an epoch now gray in the distance, down into our own broad daylight, and bringing along with it some of its legendary mist, which the reader, according to his pleasure, may either disregard, or allow it to float almost imperceptibly about the characters and events for the sake of a picturesque effect." [10]

---

[1] William Charvat, ed[et al], *The Centenary Edition of the Works of Nathaniel Hawthorne* (Columbus: Ohio State University Press, 1985) XVI:371.

[2] William Bently, *The Diary of William Bently, D.D, pastor of the East Church, Salem, Massachusetts* (Gloucester: Peter Smith, 1962) 4:71.

[3] Bentley, 2:463.

[4] Henry James, *The American Scene* (New York: St. Martin's Press, 1987), 192.

[5] ibid.

[6] Caroline Emmerton, *The Chronicle of Three Old Houses* (Published by Caroline O. Emmerton, 1935).

[7] Nathaniel Hawthorne, *The House of the Seven Gables* (New York: Bantam Books, 1981), 6.

[8] Hawthorne, 1.

[9] Hawthorne, 19.

[10] Hawthorne, vii.

The "little red cottage" in which Hawthorne wrote The House of the Seven Gables. *In the distance rises Monument Mountain where Hawthorne first met Melville in 1850. The twentieth century replica on the grounds of Tanglewood today reverses the location of the wing.*

Hawthorne Revisited
CRITICISM

"To have given your nation's literature its most persuasive representation of a woman is to have achieved genius, once and for all."
— Harold Bloom

The Scarlet Letter

By Louis Auchincloss

I suppose that one of the first things that strikes a modern reader of *The Scarlet Letter* is that its adulterous heroine, Hester Prynne, would not be considered so much of a sinner today. Consider her story. As a girl she is married off to a rich old man who is actually deformed. She is taken to a bleak new world, where her husband is captured by Indians and presumably lost forever, and she is left to her own devices in a colony where she has neither relatives nor friends. A beautiful young preacher, as silver-tongued as he is spiritual, falls in love with her, and a child is born of their guilty passion. If theirs were a sin, it nonetheless created an immortal soul.

There was, at any rate, no question about its sinfulness in the minds of the leaders of the Massachusetts Bay Colony in the fifth decade of the seventeenth century. Hawthorne was perfectly clear about this. Governor John Winthrop, who appears in the novel to die and whose shroud is woven by the heroine, recorded in his diary the actual hanging of a man and woman for adultery.

The woman proved very penitent and had deep apprehension of the foulness of her sin. The man was very much cast down for his sins, but was loath to die and petitioned for his life, but they would not grant it, though some of the magistrates questioned whether adultery was death by God's law. They were both executed; and died very penitently, especially the woman who had some comfortable hope of pardon for her sin, and gave good exhortation to all young maids to be obedient to their parents and to take heed of evil company.

Yet Hawthorne found in these stern judges and conscience-stricken adulterers the perfect laboratory in which to study guilt. Sin and guilt were almost synonymous in the Bay Colony; they fused to form darkness in the heart of man. It did not so much matter what Hester had actually done, or whether the Puritans were right or wrong in condemning her, or whether the faith of the colonists was valid or their religion true. What Hawthorne is depicting is a human soul isolated from the crowd by an act deemed foul and shameful by the community and hence by the sinner. Hester accepts her shame not so much as a judgment as a fact. It is hers; it is *she*, and she must live with it, for it has made her what she is. It is this existential element in the drama that makes it so close to us today.

The theme, the era and the setting were all perfect for Hawthorne's peculiar literary genius. His other three novels are very fine, but *The Scarlet Letter* is his masterpiece. The dark forest running down to the sea, dark as the sins of the settlers but dappled by glimpses of brilliant sunshine, somehow evoking nature's wild freedom from the moral laws of man, the grim righteousness of the Puritan elders, stern but just by their own lights, the silent bitter loneliness of the shame-accepting Hester, the demonic gaiety of her exotic child, and the redemption of the wretched Arthur Dimmesdale's soul on fire, all make a kind of literary grand opera of this superb work of art which a reader may accept with delight and even with awe, no matter how different a view he may hold of the culpability of the heroine's conduct. Call it a myth; a myth speaks to any era. One would no more judge Hester than Heathcliffe in *Wuthering Heights*.

But one can, of course, if one insists, go into the question of what Hawthorne the individual, as opposed to Hawthorne the writer, thought of the guilt of Hester and her minister. Did he share John Winthrop's view? Certainly not as to the rigor of the penalty. But there can be little doubt that he believed that theirs was a grave sin, despite all the mitigating circumstances, and that their plan to flee the new world to renew their love in Europe an equally dire one. That the community overreacted in its scornful and cruel treatment of Hester could in no way excuse her in the eyes of her author, and it may be noted that he always differentiates between the serious and disciplined elders who condemned her to wear the odious emblem of her offense and the vulgar mob who pelted her with refuse. Indeed, he goes so far as to imply that the change of mores in his own day that had brought about a more casual view of marital infidelity was a symptom of degeneration.

Here is what he has to say about the public display of Hester to the mob, adorned with her scarlet letter: "The Scene was not without a mixture of awe, such as must always invest the spectacle of guilt and shame in a fellow-creature, before society shall have grown corrupt enough to smile, instead of shuddering at it."

Yes, there was always *that* side of Hawthorne.

A NOTE ON THE AUCHINCLOSS ESSAY

By Elizabeth Hardwick

Louis Auchincloss, in his original reading of Hawthorne's mind, finds the author hostile to Hester's penalty and condemnation of the mob, but allied with the elders who viewed her adultery as a grievous sin.

Perhaps so, but the author took a risk in making Hester entrancing, dignified and noble, thereby making even the readers of the time have some difficulty being ever mindful of the seriousness of her sinning. The sin-filled, tortured Dimmesdale, a creature of his time, is less attractive. As Auchincloss suggests, Hawthorne in his life and conviction was not in every way the man at his desk. The imagination leads where it will.

Seduction and Betrayal

By Elizabeth Hardwick[1]

In *The Scarlet Letter,* has Hester Prynne been *betrayed* by the Reverend Dimmesdale? If the matter lies only inside her own feelings, perhaps we would have to say that she is beyond betrayal. Betrayal is not what she herself feels, not the way her experience shapes itself in her mind and feelings. Love, the birth of Pearl, her illegitimate child, her prison term for adultery, her sentence to wear the letter A on her breast, the insufficient courage of her lover, Dimmesdale — what provocation, what abandonment. And yet these visitations, these punishments, are embraced by Hester like fate. They are the revelations out of which prophecy is made, and so they come to her, not as depressing clouds of consequence, but as opportunities for self-knowledge, for a strange and striking *stardom.*

Dimmesdale, on the other hand, is stunned by the illicit. It corrupts the air around him; he cannot breathe because of his sin. Thinness, pallor, trembling, wasting, heartsickness: such are the words that define his state. He feels his transgression more vividly than anything else in his life. He takes society's attitude toward his adultery with Hester and, thus outcast in his own being, he becomes the betrayed person, almost the *betrayed woman.* D.H. Lawrence's idea that the "greatest triumph an American woman can have is the triumph of seducing a man, especially if he is pure" is a Lawrence paradox arising out of his suspicious dislike of Hester Prynne. It is not true that she seduced Dimmesdale, but it is true in some deep sense that the sexes are reversed in the peculiar terms of his suffering, his sinking under it, the atmosphere around him of guilt, desperation, self-torture, and lonely remorse. The weak and the strong are clearly not where we would expect them to be. Moral courage is the dominating force in Hester Prynne, just as fearfulness, neurasthenic self-abasement are the fate of Dimmesdale.

Still, it would be outside history and a psychological falsification for us to look contemptuously upon poor Dimmesdale. He is occupied with God, truly, he has his mission on earth as a clergyman. His pastorate is serious, his integration in Puritan society is passionate. He is a man in time, living under the dispensation of his moment and his region, Boston, 1642. We cannot condemn his religious scruples, his Puritan dogmatism. We can understand his not wishing to remove himself, by the confession of adultery, from the possibility of bringing light and goodness to his world. It is actually Hester Prynne who is outside history. Her indifference to adultery, her staying on in Boston with her illegitimate daughter, Pearl, her defiance, the striking skepticism of her mind, the moral distance she sets between herself and the hysterias of the time — these qualities are the cause for wonder.

The heroine whose fate is defined by adulterous love is a central and enduring theme in fiction. Love and power are the landscape in which imagined destiny is lived. Power as a consequence of conventional love is suitable for comedies and for the intense dramas of the well-to-do classes and their daughters. Love destroys power in the great tragic heroines in Greek drama, in Anna Karenina, in Cleopatra. It is infinitely more complicated and mixed in the bourgeois novel. What is asked of the heroine is not always a grand passion, but a sense of reality, a curious sort of independence and honor, an acceptance of consequence that puts courage to the most searing test.

In the novel, when the heroine's history turns about a sexual betrayal, it matters whether she is the central figure in the plot or a somewhat less powerfully and less fully considered "victim" on the periphery. If she is the central figure, psychological structure seems to demand a sort of purity and innocence. Not physical innocence, but a lack of mean calculations, of vindictiveness, of self-abasing weakness. Sexual transgression loses its overwhelming character as a wrong or as a mistake when the persons have virtues of a compelling sort, or spiritual goodness, or the grandeur of endurance. The inner life of the woman matters, what she feels and has felt, the degree of her understanding of the brutal cycles of life.

The problem of creating sympathy for the woman whose destiny must run the narrow road laid out after a disastrous surrender or seduction loomed larger in the minds of authors than it needed to loom. Fiction and drama have always been drawn magnetically to this plot, to this beginning of fated complication, and the situation inevitably partakes of the universal. The experience is common — richly, painfully known, easily imagined and felt. Lust — and then, for the women, stoicism. This is the highest choice. Yet, to be a heroine, to occupy the center of the stage as a sort of incarnation of love or sexual consequence, definite enrichments, heights, intricate particularities must set the woman apart. Her fall or her fate can only be truly serious if a natural or circumstantial refinement exists.

Again Hester Prynne is odd and we wonder how Hawthorne actually looked upon her indifference to society, her radical challenge, her sexual — what to call it? — valor. Of course, Hester is not very greatly under the spell of sensuality. Instead, she is an ideologue, making by way of her adulterous isolation a stand against Puritanism. In many respects the characters in *The Scarlet Letter* are not characters at all, but large, fantastically painted playing cards. Symbolic action is Hester's role.

Prison, where the novel starts, is a natural school for radicals, especially for those of a theatrical disposition. And Hester Prynne is very much of that sort, a dramatic, theatrical radical. Another radical moralist of the time, Anne Hutchinson, is mentioned early in the book — a woman, banished, rejected, defiant. The two are united in their public characters: Anne Hutchinson begins where Hester ends, working on the minds of troubled women, nursing the sick. And indeed what is Hester's strength except a "covenant of Grace," and a "peculiar indwelling of the Holy Ghost" of the kind Anne Hutchinson laid claim to: both make the claim of personal experience above the social or doctrinal. "What we did had a consecration of its own," Hester says.

Hester is beautiful, dark-haired, dignified, a morally complicated woman who gradually takes on a "marble coldness." She seems dramatically uninterested in religion, just as she is strikingly free in her mind about adultery. "She assumed a freedom of speculation, then common enough on the other side of the Atlantic, but which our forefathers had they known it would have held a deadlier crime than that stigmatized by the scarlet letter." The essential decision of Hester's is "I will not speak," she will not implicate Dimmesdale. She refuses any of the self-saving possibilities — but why? Her "open ignominy" has a life of its own, growing out of the peculiar strength of *the heroine* as a general literary conception. Hester, actually, is in the classical mode: she has a fate rather than a character.

Henry James: "In spite of the relation between Hester Prynne and Arthur Dimmesdale no story of love was surely ever less of a 'love story.' To Hawthorne's imagination the fact that these two persons had loved each other too well was of an interest comparatively vulgar; what appealed to him was the idea of their moral situation in the long years that were to follow." *The Scarlet Letter* is a drama of sin rather than of love. To Hester the idea that adultery is a crime is scarcely considered; she does not seem prepared to make a stand for "love" or for the purity of her feelings. She is not an apostle for sex. She is a "wild Indian" and, as Hawthorne says, with no reverence left for clerics, judges, gallows, fireside, or the church. It is not against her punishment that she flings herself — "the tendency of her fate and her fortune had been to set her free." She is a natural outcast of the superior sort: serious, somewhat vain of her dignified, sly endurance, attached to the symbolic and emblematic in the usual way of a radical wanting to signify ideas in an outward, concentrated way as he walks among the mass. It is true, as Lawrence says in fury, that she wears her damned A like a duchess's coronet. Everything about her is marvelously dramatic and challenging.

Of course, Hester cannot take the wickedness of adultery seriously because it has brought her little Pearl. Pearl is serious, living is serious, and from the natural pessimism of women with their "imprisonment" in consequence she draws a natural reprieve from the kind of moral lingering in the past that afflicts Dimmesdale. Pearl, her future, the far-flung, unknown life stretching out ahead of the sin: these mean nothing to Dimmesdale. He lingers back, preoccupied with the dead action, the fascination of transgression, the fearful power of it. He is truly in a state of lunacy, as Hester sees when they meet in the forest among the Indians. Little Pearl, with her "hard, metallic luster," is a true child of the Puritan inclination to worry the wound. She has no morals at all. She has very early leaped onto another level of possibility and will live it through without remorse or fearfulness. She becomes the glowing American girl abroad, sending home letters "with armorial seals upon them, though of bearings unknown to English heraldry." Out of this tale of repression and sorrow, of social isolation, spiritual torment, and historical hypocrisy, Hawthorne created two women with fanatical stamina, with an independence of mind and action that went beyond anything the world could rightly have asked of them in their time — or later. Mrs. Hawthorne said, when the book was read aloud to her, that she liked it but it gave her a headache.

[1] The thoughts on *The Scarlet Letter* were originally written for the collection of essays; *Seduction and Betrayal*, Random House, 1974.

What Hawthorne Meant to Melville

By Harrison Hayford

With introductory comments by Hershel Parker

INTRODUCTION

Harrison Hayford's "Melville and Hawthorne: A Biographical and Critical Study" (1945) was one of the great Yale dissertations on Melville directed by Stanley T. Williams (then fresh from writing his two-volume biography of Washington Irving). In his rigorous research Hayford discovered many unknown letters and other documents now so familiar that few people remember who found them. Among his contributions was a cautiously documented list of eight known times the men met between August 1850 and November 1851, when Melville was writing *Moby-Dick* and Hawthorne was writing *The House of the Seven Gables*.

Kept a noncombatant in World War II by tuberculosis, Hayford was so diffident about pushing ahead of colleagues who had been in the military that he refused Professor Williams's offer to publish the dissertation in the elegant, unpretentious series, "Yale Studies in English." Aside from letters of Sophia Hawthorne published by Eleanor Melville Metcalf in *Herman Melville: Cycle and Epicycle* (1953), so few new documents about the relationship between the two men emerged in the next decades that Hayford's dissertation could have been published any year up through

the 1970s with only minimal updating. Withholding distinguished work
from publication became habitual with Hayford; only in 2003 did North-
western University Press publish his *Melville's Prisoners*, a collection of
essays and speeches supervised by his son Charles Hayford and Alma
MacDougall Reising, with a foreword that I had written.

The recovery of a portion of the papers of Melville's sister Augusta in
1983 initiated a new era of research on Hawthorne, as well as Melville, in
which Hayford became a delighted witness and commentator. Carefully
examining Melville's efforts to persuade Hawthorne to write the "Agatha"
story, Hayford had challenged the claim that Melville himself had
forsworn writing after *Pierre* (1852). My discovery, half a century later,
that Melville had in fact completed the story himself — as "The Isle of
the Cross" — gave Hayford both vindication and stimulation.

In a Massachusetts paper I had found a letter written from Lenox by
"Maherbal" about Hawthorne and reprinted from the Windsor, Vermont,
Journal. My five-year hunt for the newspaper (not extant, said the
Library of Congress), ended with Richard E. Winslow's locating a file of
the paper for me. Unsurprisingly, in yet another letter from Lenox the
correspondent had relayed more gossip about Berkshire celebrities. The
quotation that follows is from my *The New Melville Log*, an expansion of
Jay Leyda's *The Melville Log*:

WINDSOR, VT January 16, 1852 The Journal *prints Maherbal's letter, "G. P.
R. JAMES — HERMAN MELVILLE," written from Lenox on January 10*:
> As may be gathered from the fact that Melville dedicated his book
> lately published to Nathaniel Hawthorne, "in admiration of his
> genius," the two distinguished writers of fiction are personal friends
> — not however familiar, intimate friends by any means — for if
> the complaints on the part of the Pittsfield people with regard
> to the exclusiveness of the one, and the representations of Maherbal
> in the Journal concerning the social character of the other, are to
> be taken as conclusive in the matter, they seem to be alike strangers
> to any thing like familiarity of social intercourse. Not very long
> ago, the author of the "Scarlet Letter" and the author of "Typee,"
> having, in some unaccountable way, gotten a mutual desire to see
> one another, as if neither had a home to which he could invite the
> other, made arrangements in a very formal manner to dine together

at a hotel in this village. What a solemn time they must have had,
those mighty conjurors in the domain of the imagination, all alone
in the dining-room of a hotel! In the small talk of the flippant beaux
and light-headed belles of Berkshire, the solemn attempt of two of
the greatest characters of which the county could boast, towards an
acquaintance, was made a subject of infinite merriment.

Baffled by conflicting evidence, Hayford nevertheless had speculated
reasonably that the men might have met for Melville to give Hawthorne
a copy of *Moby-Dick*. Decades later, from Maherbal's ignorant but
specific document, I recovered the sacred scene in which Melville presented a copy of *Moby-Dick* to its dedicatee at their last meeting in the
Berkshires. "A real DIAMOND of a find," Hayford rejoiced in his minute
criticism of a printout of that scene, praising while pushing for a clearer
visualizing of Hawthorne and Melville at the table in the dining room of
the hotel. Hayford then excitedly filled the back of the last page, starting
a third of the way down the left side and raying out east, north, and south,
here transcribed in order of inscription:

1:15 a.m. 17 July 95 Reader (HH) at end of book after the past 10
days' day & night session. Surpassingly GOOD! — this whole last
Chapter (A WOWZER — even & esp. to us old Shipmate
Melvilleans) — THAR SHE BREACHES (to high heaven) etc. etc.

But do labor, up to the moment when you surrender the last
page proofs, to polish the whole passage and this [final] paragraph
to its full shining climatic peak.

Every word counts — as in a lyric poem, which this paragraph is (it
breaks into SONG — a Song of jubilation & Praise) . . . (I'm carried
away — as I've been all week in this HOUSE and the presence of the
author of this stunningly magnificent biography.)

I print this here as a memorable record of the lifelong response to
new details about Melville and Hawthorne by the man who had pio-
neered the recovery of documentary records of their acquaintance and
had striven to capture the essential qualities of their relationship. I print
it, also, as an illustration of how great lifelong scholarship, like Hayford's
work on Hawthorne and Melville, can become part of an ongoing
collaboration of scholars, as when Hawthorne surprised both Hayford

and me by coming back onstage so often in the first draft of the second volume of my biography, which Hayford read before reading the first volume. My *Herman Melville: A Biography*, Hayford knew very well, would not have been written without "Melville and Hawthorne."

In the passage which follows, Chapter 6, section 3 of "Melville and Hawthorne," Hayford takes as a given that Hawthorne played some role in "Melville's new conception of the whaling book." In this Hayford did not directly underwrite the "two Moby-Dicks" theory of the composition of the book, first advanced in the 1940s to account for the book's being called mostly done in the summer of 1850 yet not finished until the summer of 1851. According to a rough-and-ready simplification of the theory, Melville first wrote a book of whaling adventure then, under the influence of Shakespeare, or under the influence of Hawthorne (or something else), rewrote it as a philosophical tragedy.

Aware that Melville habitually stuffed into his books material he could not have intended to put there all along, Hayford was nevertheless alert to the momentum a powerful creative process gains as it propels itself toward a conclusion. Long afterward, in "Unnecessary Duplicates: A Key to the Writing of Moby-Dick" (1978) Hayford from internal evidence elaborated a theory based in part on the obvious shift in which Melville dropped Ishmael's momentous companion, Bulkington, the stalwart helmsman, in favor of Queequeg, the exotic harpooneer. As I revised the Norton Critical Edition in 2001, I worked in documentary evidence from a young scholar, Geoffrey Sanborn, that Melville had based Queequeg closely upon Tupai Cupa, a real man described in George Lillie Craik's *The New Zealanders* (1830), a book no Melvillean had ever heard about. Now one has to assume that sometime in 1850 (May? June? later?) Melville laid hand on Craik's book and saw, at once, some (but not all) of the wondrous things he might do with Tupai Cupa. All this came too late for Hayford to understand, but in his full powers he would have taken topgallant delight in pondering the ramifications of Sanborn's discovery. No one took more delight than Hayford when a younger scholar struck gold, even in a stream he had himself panned.

The notion of Hawthorne's possible influence on *Moby-Dick* runs through the following paragraphs, Hayford's elegant and eloquent summation of the ways Melville responded to Hawthorne during this crucial year in both their lives. The passage that follows is characteristic of

Hayford in that he shows Melville and Hawthorne as working writers, living their lives as they wrote, open to impressions, from books, from people, from the air. The word "influence" in Hayford carried its Latin vividness; he thought in terms of processes. (Quotations are left as they were in 1945, not collated to texts Hayford later supervised in his ongoing study of the documents.)

> — Hershel Parker
> September 2003
> *Morro Bay, California*

———

Melville and Hawthorne:
A Biographical and Critical Study (Excerpt)

By Harrison Hayford

Were Hawthorne and his writings reagents, or catalysts, in whatever complex reaction it was that precipitated Melville's new conception of the whaling book? The question cannot be answered with the mechanical assurance of scientific fact. In the subtle chemistry of mind we cannot balance all equations, and we have no control experiments. Even an affidavit signed by Melville himself might not give an unchallengeable answer. Still, there is sufficient evidence that Hawthorne and his writings were indeed involved in this reaction.

To begin with, there is no doubt that Melville was receptive to outside influences. For the past four years, he told Hawthorne, his mind had been unfolding within itself like a growing plant and there was scarcely a three-weeks' period when he was not conscious of development and change. The comparison he draws between his mind and an unfolding plant must not be allowed to suggest that his mind put forth only what was latent within itself, that its efflorescence was unaffected by outer weather. No doubt some inner necessity, or some complex of influences indistinguishable from the "mind" itself, determined the direction and course of his development from *Typee* through to *Billy Budd*.

Yet nothing in his career is plainer to read than the sensitivity of his mind to outer weather, at least up to the time of *Pierre*. In his three years in New York, it was immensely stimulated and enriched by his association with Duyckinck and his literary circle; by his reflections upon the social and political ferment at home and abroad, the struggles of emerging democracy, the anti-slavery agitation, the war with Mexico, the revolutions of 1848; by his discovery of "the world of mind," his lynx-eyed reading in Plato, Rabelais, Browne, Burton, Shakespeare, ancient and modern history, and contemporary science; by his attendance at the opera, the theater and the art galleries; by his eager exploration of the old enigmas of philosophy; by his assumption of the responsibilities of marriage and family life; and by his experience of authorship, its wine of inspired composition and its pot-boiling drudgery, the elation of public acclaim and the sting of stupid criticism. His voyage to England in 1849, intense weeks saturated in the sights and sounds of London, then a glimpse of the Continent, including post-war Paris, and the return to London where he experienced what the highest contemporary literary and artistic companionship might be like, joined together to confirm his sense of himself as a writer in the long British tradition. All these fertilizing experiences (and others) had stimulated and shaped the growth of his mind and passed into the substance of what he wrote.

Melville's mind was unfolding rapidly, but in doing so it was not unaffected by outside influences. There is good enough reason to infer that Hawthorne as man and author, coming into Melville's ken at this crucial time, played a real part in the sea-change whereby the original whaling book was transformed into something rich and strange. Melville's own writings, if not his signed affidavit, testify to Hawthorne's importance to him during the months when the change was being effected.

In the first place, there is the abounding joy of Melville's discovery of Hawthorne's *Mosses*, to which his essay on the book bears such eloquent and generous witness. Reading *Mosses from an Old Manse* he found note after note in it that vibrated in harmony with some chord in his own thought. Hawthorne's rich humor, his spirit of love for all created things, his great, deep intellect plumbing the depths of truth, his sudden flashes of insight, his union of head and heart, these were the very qualities that Melville so greatly admired in Shakespeare and that he would seek to make his own in *Moby-Dick*; Hawthorne's *Mosses*, moreover, justified his hope for a great American literature and renewed his ambition to contribute to its fullness. Already, he felt, Hawthorne had "dropped germanous seeds" into his soul — seeds to germinate, we may believe, in *Moby-Dick*. After his discovery of the *Mosses*, there is Melville's continued delight in Hawthorne's books, expressed in his letters during the ensuing months. In the *Twice-Told Tales* he found "meanings worthy of a Brahmin" and from *The House of the Seven Gables* he garnered deep matter for "a whole year of thoughtfulness."

In the letters, too, there is Melville's continued identification of his own views with those of Hawthorne, an identification that constantly tends to become personal and reveals the intimate connection in Melville's mind between Hawthorne the author and Hawthorne the man. He not only identified his views with those of Hawthorne, but often, one feels, projected himself as Hawthorne. He pictured Hawthorne "up to the lips in the Universe." He spoke of "men like you and me, and some others, forming a chain of God's posts around the world." And analyzing "the purport and significance of what so strongly characterizes all of this author's writings," he saw him as "the man who, like Russia or the British Empire, declares himself as sovereign nature (in himself) amid the powers of Heaven, hell, and earth. He may perish; but so long as he exists he insists on treating with all Powers upon an equal basis."

Continuing the analysis, he betrayed the unconscious identification by shifting insensibly from "he" to "me." "If any of those other Powers choose to withhold certain secrets, let them; that does not impair my sovereignty in myself; that does not make me tributary." Surely, this is Ahab, or a mood of Melville, rather than Hawthorne; and surely, too, it is Melville, not Hawthorne, who says "No" in thunder.

The identification reached a conscious climax in the final letter of the Berkshire year, in which, in his delight that Hawthorne had understood his book, Melville waxed pantheistic: "Whence come you, Hawthorne? By what right do you drink from my flagon of life? And when I put it to my lips — lo, they are yours and not mine. I feel that the Godhead is broken up like the bread at the Supper, and that we are the pieces. Hence this infinite fraternity of feeling." Noting this projection and identification, critics have frequently observed that Melville saw Hawthorne in his own image; and the observation is true, but only partly true. Everything we admire is likely to be both what we half create and what we perceive; and the important thing is that Melville was moved and influenced by Hawthorne, whether by what he saw or what he thought he saw.

Other things in the letters show that Hawthorne, personally, meant much to Melville during these months. In the years just past, his letters to Duyckinck were written with an easy familiarity and sometimes spoke frankly enough about his literary ambitions and his disappointments; his letters to Dana show him reaching out for friendship with another writer and delighting in the thought that Dana, in reading *Redburn* and *White-Jacket*, had experienced the same strange, congenial feelings with which he himself had read *Two Years Before the Mast* and felt "tied and welded" to the author "by a sort of Siamese link of affectionate sympathy." In none of his other letters, however, did he write with such unreserve as in the letters to Hawthorne. That he talked with the same confident unreserve in conversation with Hawthorne, Mrs. Hawthorne testifies, at a later date: "Mr. Melville, generally silent and incommunicative, pours out the rich floods of his mind and experience to him, so sure of apprehension, so sure of a large and generous interpretation, and of the most delicate and fine judgment." Melville writes to Hawthorne frankly, of himself, his ideas, of his book. He writes of the pleasure he takes in their meetings when they discuss the universe with cigars and a bottle of brandy, and the letters probably furnish a good enough sample of the nature of the conversations. However infrequent their meetings, Melville evidently felt confident of Hawthorne's understanding, and it was such confidence he needed to encourage him to write a book of truth.

Finally, Melville's dedication to Hawthorne of the book upon which he had expended so much labor and time and thought is a tribute to Hawthorne's genius and an acknowledgment of what its example had meant to Melville while he slaved on the book.

A Moonlight Visibility:

Turning *The Scarlet Letter* into a play

By Carol Gilligan

Moonlight, in a familiar room, falling so white upon the carpet, and showing all its figures so distinctly,— making every object so minutely visible, yet so unlike a morning or noontide visibility. . . .
— Hawthorne. *The Scarlet Letter*

It was the death of his mother that impelled Hawthorne to write *The Scarlet Letter.* As a child he had seen his mother scorned by his father's family after his father, a sea captain, died in Surinam when Nathaniel was four. Raised by his mother who took him and his sisters and went back to live with her family, Hawthorne was brought up in a household of women. Following his graduation from Bowdoin College, he lived for twelve years in his mother's house, teaching himself to write. But it was only with *The Scarlet Letter* that he managed to still a critical, censorious voice inside him, reflecting subsequently in his journal, "I think I have never overcome my own adamant in any other instance."

Hawthorne calls *The Scarlet Letter* a romance, a blending of the actual and the imaginary. It also has the character of a dream, its manifest content concealing its latent meanings. Setting his story in seventeenth century Boston, Hawthorne draws on historical figures — the Reverend John Wilson, Governor Bellingham, and Mistress Hibbins who was burned as a witch — to establish "an iron framework of reasoning," a powerful alliance of church and state where "law and religion were almost identical," a patriarchal world where women were divided into "goodwives" and witches. Within this framework, he places the triangle of Hester Prynne, her lover Arthur Dimmesdale, and her husband — the man who calls himself Roger Chillingworth. At its center, Pearl, the luminous child whose existence reveals her mother's "lawless passion," becomes the voice of emotional truth in a world where such truths cannot be spoken.

Seen in a morning or noontide light, Hester has committed the crime and sin of adultery. The magistrates, moved by compassion — thinking that her husband, missing for two years, is likely at the bottom of the sea and seeing that she was young and fair and doubtless was strongly tempted — have waived the penalty of death, ruling instead that she wear a scarlet A as a badge of shame. Arthur Dimmesdale, the pious young Reverend who has "done a wild thing," the favorite son of the Puritan fathers, appears in the eyes of the Puritans as Christ-like in his embrace of suffering, while Chillingworth appears as a fiend in seeking to worm his way into the minister's heart. Within this Christian world-view, Pearl is seen as a wild and unruly child.

In naming Hester's lover and husband Dimmesdale and Chillingworth, Hawthorne invites us to consider how two men, described as unusually sensitive and perceptive, come to inhabit these identities. Chillingworth was "a wise and just man," devoting his life to "the advancement of human welfare." Held captive by the Indians, he learned from them the healing powers of nature, and bringing these skills into the Puritan settlement, he became a skilled physician. Dimmesdale was revered by his congregation, a man singled out for his intelligence. But as a noontide perception gives way to a moonlight visibility, Hester defines a radical shift in perception.

Dimmesdale's embrace of suffering becomes an evasion, a betrayal of love, ironically in the name of the Heavenly Father. Chillingworth, however fiend-like in his pursuit of Dimmesdale, is also the one who says that Hester should not be standing alone on the scaffold, who attends to the screaming infant, providing a remedy that calms her and one for her mother as well; in the end, he becomes like a father to Pearl in a way that was previously unimagined, leaving her all his money and property which were considerable and thus freeing her to lead her own life. And Hester, seeking and gaining Chillingworth's release from her promise to conceal his identity, turns the Puritan world-view on its head. "My sin," she says, "was to enter into this marriage when I felt no love. And his crime was to persuade me to fancy myself happy by his side, at a time when my heart knew no better."

A morality play has given way to a psychological drama, and it was this drama I sought to stage when Tina Packer of Shakespeare & Company invited me to transpose Hawthorne's romance into a play. In overcoming his adamant, Hawthorne did what Virginia Woolf would do in killing "the angel in the house." He silenced an internalized voice that had kept him from saying what he saw. The challenges I faced in writing the play lay in dramatizing the radical shifts in perception and revealing the emotional subtext that drives the characters and their actions.

A stands for adultery, but it also comes to mean "able" as Hester is seen as more of a woman than the "goodwives" of Puritanism: "Such helpfulness was found in her — so much power to do, and power to sympathize — that many people refused to interpret the scarlet A by its original signification. They said it meant Able; so strong was Hester Prynne, with a woman's strength." Living outside the framework of Puritanism, Hester sees the frame. "Is the world then so narrow?" she asks the anguished Dimmesdale, a man whose "genuine impulse" was to adore the truth, yet who was living a lie. "Doth the universe lie within the compass of yonder town, which only a little time ago was but a leaf-strewn desert?"

It was an age in which "the human intellect, newly emancipated, had taken a more active and a wider range than for many centuries before. Men of the sword had overthrown nobles and kings. Men bolder than these had overthrown and rearranged — not actually, but within the sphere of theory…the whole system of ancient prejudice, wherewith was linked much of ancient principle." As Hester roams the forest on the edge of the settlement, her mind runs free, "casting off the fragments of a broken chain." Charged by Providence with raising a daughter, she

questions the ancient prejudices and principles that govern the relationship between man and woman, dividing her from Dimmesdale and
Dimmesdale from himself, restricting her ability to cultivate in her
daughter "the germ and blossom of womanhood," and restraining women
from assuming "what would seem to be a fair and suitable position" in
the new society.

Color defines the contrast between Hester and the goodwives: she is
radiant, her hair dark and abundant, the scarlet letter embroidered bril-
liantly in red and gold thread; they are gray and pale. Hester sees that
"the whole race of womanhood" and "the very nature of the opposite
sex, or its long hereditary habit which has become like nature," are in
reality part of a "system of society" that, built up in one way, could be
"torn down and built up anew." Such speculation, the narrator tells us,
would have been held by our forefathers to be "a deadlier crime than that
stigmatized by the scarlet letter." Freeing her sexuality, Hester released
herself from the constraints of Puritanism; from this vantage point, she
sees "the foundations of the Puritan establishment" as a human construction, neither divinely ordained nor natural.

The Scarlet Letter was written in 1850, at the height of Abolitionist
Feminism. Hawthorne had married Sophia Peabody, whose older sister
Elizabeth was among its leading activists. While Hawthorne, at least in
his noontide presentation, was neither an abolitionist nor a feminist, the
word "patriarchy" runs through "The Custom House," the introductory
sketch he appends to his romance: "patriarchal body of veterans;" "the
father of the Custom House — the patriarch;" "this patriarchal
personage…[who] was, in truth, a rare phenomenon; so perfect, in one
point of view, so shallow, so delusive, so impalpable, such an absolute
nonentity in every other." The word returns when Dimmesdale ("the
minister in a maze") considers telling the truth: "patriarchal privilege,"
"the sanctified old patriarchal deacon." It is clear what is at stake. And
Hester protects Dimmesdale's position, not only at her own expense
but also at the expense of her relationship with her daughter, the
luminous Pearl.

Pearl's "remarkable precocity and acuteness" encourage Hester to see
her as someone whom she could entrust "with as much of her mother's
sorrows as could be imparted, without irreverence either to the parent or
the child." And yet when Pearl's searching questions open the way to such

a relationship, Hester holds back. She sees emerging in Pearl's strong emotions and character the "sterling attributes" of a "noble woman…the stedfast principles of an unflinching courage — an uncontrollable will, — a sturdy pride, which might be disciplined into self-respect, — and a bitter scorn of many things which, when examined, might be found to have the taint of falsehood in them." And yet paradoxically, to keep Pearl with her, she must distance herself from her and educate her daughter to live within the bounds of a Puritanical order.

The music of the Puritans — the certain harmonies and serene majesty of their hymns — offered a way to evoke the experience and allure of living within an all-encompassing worldview. Struggling to find a sufficient counterweight, I was drawn by Hester's conflict, familiar through my research with women, and also to the voice of Pearl that rang true to my experience in working with girls. I fleshed out the relationship between Hester and Pearl to show their playfulness and joy with one another and built the first act around the tension between emotional truth and "an iron framework of reasoning" — a tension that culminates in a series of lies. Dimmesdale lies to Chillingworth, Chillingworth lies to Dimmesdale, and Hester lies to Pearl who becomes hysterical.

"Mother," Pearl asks "what does the scarlet letter mean?" "Mother! — Mother! — Why does the minister keep his hand over his heart?" She has made the connection nobody was supposed to see.

"What shall I say?" Hester asks herself.

"Silly Pearl," she says, "what questions are these? There are many things in this world that a child must not ask about. What know I of the minister's heart? And as for the scarlet letter, I wear it for the sake of its gold thread!" She cannot tell Pearl what Pearl intuitively knows, cannot allow her to know it for fear that the child will be taken away from her: "Hold thy tongue, naughty child!", she says, "Do not tease me; else I shall shut thee into the dark closet!" Act I ends with Pearl throwing herself on the floor and screaming.

In the second act, I depart from Hawthorne's text to show what he only alludes to: the love between Hester and Dimmesdale, Dimmesdale's Election Day sermon that electrifies the congregation, and Pearl as a young woman living in Italy — the parts of the story the narrator excludes in summarizing it as "a tale of human frailty and sorrow."

Hester is introduced at the beginning of the novel as a sensual and spirited young woman, tall, "with a figure of perfect elegance, on a large scale;" the scarlet A that she embroiders "so fantastically" illuminates her, "taking her out of the ordinary relations with humanity, and inclosing her in a sphere by herself." By the end of the novel, she is the woman to whom other women come for comfort and counsel in love, "demanding why they were so wretched, and what the remedy?" She assures them of her "firm belief that at some brighter period, when the world has grown ripe for it, in Heaven's own time, a new truth would be revealed in order to establish the whole relation between man and woman on a surer ground of mutual happiness." For a time she imagined that she might be the prophetess of this revelation, bringing the truth that would establish a new order of living, but she "had long since recognized the impossibility."

Hawthorne's insight into Hester's predicament is brilliant. With the economy of the single letter "A," he captures how the very passion that enables a woman to free herself from the iron framework of patriarchy also disables her by causing her to be seen, in the eyes of the Puritans, as an impure woman, a woman who has been adulterated. "A" means adultery, "A" means able, "A" means angel and apostle; the novel floats all these possibilities and then draws its somber conclusion: "The angel and apostle of the coming revelation must be a woman, indeed," but she must be lofty and pure as well as beautiful and wise, not through "dusky grief" but through the ethereal joy of sacred love. The very possibility turns out to be impossible, at least within the world of the novel. But while Hester cannot free her lover, the aptly named Dimmesdale, she does succeed in freeing her daughter who by the end of the novel is living in Italy.

I wrote the love scene in the forest to show the passion between Dimmesdale and Hester when they rekindle their love and plan to leave the Puritan settlement. With Tina Packer who directed the play, I puzzled over the question Dimmesdale asks once he grasps the possibility of embracing joy: "Why did we not find it sooner?" Since Hester's husband was presumed to be dead and Dimmesdale was unmarried, why hadn't they left, why didn't they marry? Dimmesdale's character posed the most difficult challenge for us and also for the actors who struggled to find him sympathetic. Tina and I wrestled with the question of how to understand his internal struggle, how to dramatize his conflict, or even how to ask the question.

I wrote Dimmesdale's Election Day sermon in response to this challenge. In the forest when Dimmesdale encounters Hester — their first time alone in seven years, his manhood returns and his body is restored to health. Standing in "a flood of sunshine," they see their love as having "a consecration of its own." Returning home, Dimmesdale flings the sermon he prepared into the fire and writes another with the same "impulsive flow of thought and emotion" that Hawthorne experienced in writing *The Scarlet Letter*. I saw Dimmesdale's epiphany as a radical insight into Christianity that dissolved the tension between his ministry and his manhood: if God is love, how can love be sin?

I imagined he would buttress this perception with Scripture, citing the Gospel of John: "He that dwelleth in love, dwelleth in God, and God in him." In confessing his sin, he would seek to take his congregation with him, reminding them that when Christ said, "He that is without sin, let him cast the first stone at her," he was speaking of a woman taken in adultery. It was Pearl, the little child, who had sought to lead him to this place, urging him to turn a moonlight visibility into a noontide vision by standing with Hester and with her not only at night or in the forest but in the marketplace in the full light of day. But it is a vision that he cannot sustain.

At the end of Act II, as the light fades on the dying minister, Hester rises and leaves him, taking off her Puritan cap and joining Pearl who stands at the front of the stage. The music shifts from the Puritan hymn, "O Bless the Lord My Soul," to the contemporary, "Uncommon Ritual" as Hester removes Pearl's Puritan costume and a young woman wearing a simple but elegant black dress appears in the place of the girl.

I wrote an epilogue for Pearl. "We left," she says, "my mother and I, shortly after my father's death." She grew up in England and went to live in Italy when Hester returned to Boston, "hiding her bright hair under a Puritan cap, donning her old gray dress, and yes, the scarlet letter." Hester's counsel to the Puritan women in the novel becomes her benediction for her daughter in the play; stating her conviction that a new truth will ground the relation between man and woman not in sorrow but in happiness, Hester kisses Pearl and leaves.

A swing comes down where the platform of the pillory stood, and as Pearl begins to swing, a young man enters, dressed in Italian slacks and an open shirt. He stands behind her, pushing her higher. They laugh, and when she gets off the swing, they embrace.

"We have a daughter," Pearl says, "a wild and unruly Sophia. Today is her birthday." Like Pearl in the play, she is seven years old.

Hawthorne sees into the structure of patriarchy with a clarity that few modern writers have attained. He sees its effects on sensitive men, rendering one dim and the other chilling, and also on relations between mothers and daughters, restraining a mother from affirming her daughter's perceptions or telling her what she knows about men and love. How astonishingly modern this 1850 novel is; as I write, a woman in Nigeria, accused of adultery, is in danger of being stoned to death in accordance with the law of Sharia. An alliance of church and state is solidifying in many parts of the world, encouraging a militant fundamentalism and supported by "an iron framework of reasoning."

The voice of what Hawthorne in a seemingly contemporary vocabulary refers to as the "inner man" or "profounder self" is the voice that exposes the iron framework, revealing its hypocrisies and its lies. But the shift in framework confuses the ability to distinguish the real from the imagined: "No man, for any considerable period, can wear one face to himself, and another to the multitude, without finally getting bewildered as to which may be the true." Hawthorne presents conflicting accounts of what happened that day on the scaffold when Dimmesdale exposed the place over his heart where he had kept his hand. Some said they had seen a scarlet letter identical to Hester's imprinted on his flesh. Others denied there was any mark whatever. The official version was that the minister, "by yielding up his breath in the arms of that fallen woman," had made of his death a parable, conveying "the mournful and mighty lesson, that, in the view of Infinite Purity, we are sinners all alike." The reader is left to "choose among these many theories."

I choose to go with Hester, to resist the allure of the *pieta*, to follow the inspiration of Jason Fitzgerald who designed the sound for the Shakespeare & Company production in modulating the strains of the Puritan Hymm into the brighter sounds of "Uncommon Ritual." In the forest, when Hester undoes the clasp that fastened the scarlet letter and throws it among the withered leaves, she experiences an "exquisite relief. She had not known the weight, until she felt the freedom!" When she removes the cap that confined her hair, "her sex, her youth, and the whole richness of her beauty, came back from what men call the irrevocable past." Love "had been aroused" from a death-like slumber. Unclouding

Dimmesdale's vision by revealing the possibility of leaving "these iron men and their opinions," Hester challenges him to give up the name of Arthur Dimmesdale and to make himself a brighter one.

I read *The Scarlet Letter* as a letter written by Hawthorne to his mother after her death, expressing what he could not say to her — or perhaps even know — while she was living. In the character of Hester Prynne, he reveals his insight into her situation; in Pearl he captures a child's perception and also the pressures on the child not to see or say what is true. In Dimmesdale and Chillingworth, he exposes the vulnerabilities of men whose artistic sensibilities are dulled or frozen by the strictures of a patriarchal order. His moonlit romance thus becomes an epitaph of sorts, a benediction for his mother, and also perhaps an act of self-forgiveness for the extent to which he had stood apart. It carries the recognition or perhaps the wish that the very nature of man or what through long hereditary habit had come to seem like human nature could be essentially modified, that woman could assume a fair and suitable position in a reconstructed society, and that relationships between man and woman could be established on a surer ground of mutual happiness.

*Lillian Gish and Lars Hanson
in the 1926 silent film version of
The Scarlet Letter.*

*Colleen Moore and
Hardie Albright
1934.*

*Demi Moore and
Gary Oldman
1995.*

The Scarlet Letter: Movies and Television

By Neil Hickey

T*he Scarlet Letter* has been dramatized for film and television more often than any other classic work of American letters — a dozen attempts including silent versions in 1913 and 1926, an early talkie in 1934, German director Wim Wenders' 1972 effort (*Der Scarlachrote Buchstabe*), a four-hour PBS marathon in 1979, and a lavish 1995 movie starring Demi Moore as a smoldering (and briefly nude) Hester.

None has been fully respectful of the novel, which Henry James called "the finest piece of imaginative writing yet put forth" in the New World. As a familiar literary work in the public domain, *The Scarlet Letter* is a lodestar for moviemakers unwilling or unable to pay high prices for film rights to crowd-pleasing stories, leaving Hawthorne defenseless against his dramaturgic interpreters. The novel, in its complexity, may defy dramatization, much as has *Ulysses*. In any event, a wholly satisfying film rendition remains to be made.

The best of the field so far is Lillian Gish's 1926 silent, with the respected Swedish stage actor Lars Hansen as Dimmesdale, and Henry B. Walthall as Chillingworth. (Lip readers will be frustrated; Hansen

performed all his lines in Swedish.) Movie censors in the 1920s placed
Hawthorne's novel on an unofficial blacklist as inappropriate entertainment for decent Americans. As a result, Gish was obliged to appeal to
church and women's groups to get the ban lifted; they agreed, if Gish
would "personally" assure that delicate sensibilities would not be offended
by Hester's iniquity. MGM's youthful production executive, Irving
Thalberg, chose Victor Seastrom, Sweden's most prominent moviemaker,
to direct, working with Henrik Sartov, Gish's favorite cinematographer.
Frances Marion, a leading scenario writer, won the difficult task of adapt-
ing the novel.

Moviegoers attending the film received early warning about what they
were in for. Inscribed on the first title card: "Here is recorded a stark
episode in the lives of a stern, unforgiving people, a story of bigotry
uncurbed and its train of sorrow, shame and tragedy." Departing immediately from the text, a virginal, playful Hester is shown being excoriated
by the Massachusetts Colony's guardians of public morals for being too
merry on the Sabbath; she's clamped in stocks on the pillory platform.
Dimmesdale manages to procure her freedom, and Gish's wide-eyed
effusions of gratitude and longing are easily decoded: "This is the chap
for me."

There follows an interpolated scene in which Hester washes her
underwear in the river, and to her intense embarrassment, Dimmesdale
saunters by, requiring her — by the laws of the Colony — to conceal the
garments lest they trigger concupiscent fantasies in the minister. He
catches sight of the bloomers — which do, in fact, have the dread, pre-
dicted effect on Dimmesdale. He and Hester stroll into the forest and we
are invited to assume that their union is consummated, there in the bushes
on the riverbank, and that the baby Pearl is not far in the future.

The moviemakers must then solve the self-created problem of what
to do with Dimmesdale for the next nine months, until the story can
resume its momentum. Deftly, they send him to England bearing a
message for the king from the Colony's governor. Before leaving, he
visits Hester at her cabin, asks her to marry him and accompany him on
the journey. But she breaks the news that she's already married, leaving
Dimmesdale thunderstruck, as only a lovesick minister in 1642 could be.
Hester begs him to remain in the colony and pleads for forgiveness, but
he departs angrily. In a nice bit of cinematic symbology, Hester's

spinning wheel casts its large, vivid shadow across her body like a bull's-eye. Fade out.

Thereafter, the filmmakers rejoin Hawthorne, returning to the text — with harmless extrapolations, some of them Shakespearean-style comic relief. Dimmesdale returns from England to learn he's a father. Roger "Chillingworth" (*né* Prynne) — performed with Rasputin-like menace by Walthall — makes his entrance and commences his hound-of-heaven (or hell) pursuit of Dimmesdale. Hansen's Dimmesdale is a creature of wild disarrangement as his body and mind degrade in that agony of guilt and lunacy leading to his public confession in the marketplace. Lillian Gish cradles him in her arms as he foresees "a better freedom than any we've dreamed of." He expires and hundreds of onlookers respectfully remove their conical Puritan hats, and turn and drift away.

Curiously, Colleen Moore's 1934 version (her final film) is often called "an early talkie," even as it reached movie houses fully seven years into the sound era. The acting and production values are archaic, redolent of the silent era, perhaps because its Italian-born director, Robert G. Vignola, had been a silent film actor and began his directing career in 1911. His best-known film was the 1922 costume epic *When Knighthood Was in Flower*, starring Marion Davies. Nineteen thirty-four, after all, was the year of *It Happened One Night, The Thin Man, Babes in Toyland, Great Expectations, Of Human Bondage, Jane Eyre, The Gay Divorcee, The Barretts of Wimpole Street* and scores of other technically and artistically sophisticated films. Vignola appears not to have paid attention.

Colleen Moore is miscast. Hardie Albright is too operatic as Dimmesdale, and Henry B. Walthall, sporting an even longer beard, reprises Chillingworth. Alan Hale (later a busy character actor at Warner Bros.) and William Farnum provide comic interludes not in the novel. Albright dies persuasively in the final scene. "Now I stand where I should have stood five years ago — by your side," he tells Moore. But the movie is badly paced and survives as a curio for film-history obsessives, not an entertainment for the rest of us.

Wim Wenders, early in his career, had a go at directing *The Scarlet Letter* in German, casting the beguiling Senta Berger in the lead, supported by Lou Castel as Dimmesdale and Hans-Christian Blech as Chillingworth. A better result might have been expected from the filmmaker who subsequently gave us *Wings of Desire, City of Angels,* and *The*

Buena Vista Social Club and became a favorite of foreign film enthusiasts in the U.S. His setting is a mountainous, forbidding coastline that cannot be mistaken for New England's. A too-intrusive musical score busily attempts to program the viewer's emotions. Wenders's 90-minute effort owes as much to Ingmar Bergman as to Hawthorne, but the final product has an antique realism and menace that makes it worth searching for in your local video store.

In a 1979 four-hour public television dramatization of "The Scarlet Letter" (unaccountably subtitled "A Romance") from WGBH, Boston's excellent PBS affiliate, the astonishing paleness of Meg Foster's gray eyes and her lugubrious sensuality as Hester are enough to make the version worth experiencing. Kevin Conway, similarly, is a vivid Chillingworth. John Heard's Dimmesdale is more a whipped cur than required by the text. "Hester, I have not your strength," he moans. "My teachers have been shame, despair and solitude." Rick Hauser produced and directed.

To its credit, this television version includes bits of the Custom House prefatory chapter (the only one we viewed that does so) in which Hawthorne makes a personal appearance to set the stage for Hester's story, which happened 200 years earlier. He discovers in old archives a packet of manuscript "done up in a piece of ancient yellow parchment" plus an "affair of fine red cloth, much worn and faded" in the shape of the letter "A", 3 1/4 inches high. And so the story moves to Prison Lane in Boston on a summer day as Meg Foster, infant at the bosom, emerges from the jail into bright sunlight to face the contemptuous townspeople.

Reviewing WGBH's "Letter," The Christian Science Monitor called it "four hours of overwhelmingly enjoyable literate entertainment," and in fact the adaptation (by Allan Knee and Alvin Sapinsley) is more attentive to Hawthorne's text than most — as befits a dramatization underwritten by the National Endowment for the Humanities, and other corporate and private arts supporters.

The most recent filmic *Letter* is director Roland (*The Killing Fields*) Joffe's 1995 endeavor, which bears the legend "Freely adapted from the novel by Hawthorne." Truer words rarely have been spoken. (Advertisements neglected to mention the name Hawthorne.) Still, it's the most lavishly produced (filmed in Nova Scotia), and, well, erotic of the movie versions, with an expensive cast: Demi Moore, Gary Oldman (Dimmesdale), Robert Duvall (Chillingworth), Joan Plowright (Harriet

Hibbins), and authentic-looking buildings and settings. Some of the production money appears to have come from — of all people — the late billionaire playboy Dodi Fayed, Princess Diana's final companion, who is listed as co-executive producer.

At the opening, Demi/Hester arrives in Massachusetts from England and, soon, during a stroll along the river, catches a glimpse of Dimmesdale swimming in the nude. Later, they "meet cute" on a washed out road when her wagon is stuck in the mud and he rescues her. At the Meeting House, she discovers that he is, in fact, the local minister. Contemplating him while having a bath that evening, she rises from the tub as the camera explores her dripping body — as the bodies of few seventeenth-century Puritan seamstresses have been explored.

The usually splendid Robert Duvall is defeated by the Chillingworth role, essaying an accent of undeterminable provenance, and eventually hangs himself for reasons having nothing to do with Hawthorne's intentions. Gary Oldman is better, managing a virile, credible Dimmesdale to whom Hester might logically have surrendered her virtue. The movie entertains on its own level, if one sets aside all expectations of encountering Hawthorne, or, preferably, has never read the novel.

Allusions to *The Scarlet Letter* abound in American popular culture. My favorite: Professor Harold Hill in Meredith Wilson's 1957 Broadway musical *The Music Man*, lamenting Marian the librarian's prissy, bourgeois morality. "I hope, I pray," he sings, "for Hester to win just one more A. The sadder but wiser girl for me."

Dimmesdale's Ailment, Hawthorne's Insight

By M. Gerard Fromm

"Every dream has at least one point at which it is unfathomable; a central point, as it were, connecting it with the unknown." With this epigraph, James Mellow begins his award-winning biography, *Nathaniel Hawthorne in His Times*[1]. The words are Sigmund Freud's, from *The Interpretation of Dreams*. Mellow ends his biography with Melville's belief, as conveyed by Julian Hawthorne, "that Hawthorne had all his life concealed some great secret, which would, were it known, explain all the mysteries of his career."

Hawthorne's life and work abound in mystery. He was an attractive, but elusive person: a combination of reserve, coolness, gentility and unexpected attentiveness that could transfix the other person in a middle distance of interest, loyalty and unsatisfied desire. After his death, his wife, Sophia, said that he "veiled himself from himself. I never dared gaze at him ... It seemed an invasion into a holy place ... (H)e was ... to me a divine Mystery ... "[2]

The mysteries of *The Scarlet Letter* are themselves many and a major source of the novel's power. It is at once a romance, a tragedy and an allegory, dense with symbolism and themes that can be read historically, biblically, even clinically. From that latter angle, a number of questions invite examination. How did Hawthorne know about psychosomatic illness — Dimmesdale's ailment — fifty years before Freud? How might we think about his startling descriptions of the treatment relationship and of child development? Does a clinical perspective on his life history contribute anything to an understanding of the text?

———

Arthur Dimmesdale, is suffering; he is pale, emaciated, melancholic and progressively weakened by pain. His will to live is fading. He is eventually treated by the physician, Roger Chillingworth, with whom Hawthorne sets up that basic tension between faith and science pervading Western culture since the fourteenth century. "In (a doctor's) researches into the human frame, it may be that the higher ... faculties of such men were materialized, and ... lost the spiritual view of existence amid the intricacies of that wondrous mechanism..."[3] On the other hand, "(t)here was a fascination for the minister in the company of the man of science, in whom he recognized an intellectual cultivation ... together with a range and freedom of ideas, that he would have vainly looked for among the members of his own profession."[4] Dimmesdale's faith, "supporting, while it confined him," met in Chillingworth "a window ... admitting a freer atmosphere into the close and stifled study, where his life was wasting away ... "[5]

To be a doctor implies healing, but "to doctor" can mean to adulterate, i.e., to make impure by the mixing in of foreign or inferior elements. The American Psychological Association would certainly have affixed a scarlet A upon Dr. Chillingworth for his breach of professional ethics, because he adulterated his therapeutic role with another role, that of wronged husband, and he allowed a murderous counter-transference to mix with an initially therapeutic attitude. For Dimmesdale, Chillingworth's doctoring not only risks the revelation of his sin; it risks transforming the higher order of spirit into faithless materiality, a form of reverse alchemy. If Chillingworth were actually offering therapeutic understanding, would that absolve Dimmesdale of moral responsibility?

Adulteration or corruption — and both the hope for and fear of transformation — is a central theme of *The Scarlet Letter*, represented in

Chillingworth's doctoring and Dimmesdale's ministry, and enacted, though never named as adultery, in Hester's drama. Hawthorne had just experienced his own personal struggle with corruption, at two levels: first, his politically-motivated dismissal from his position in the Salem Customs House on allegations of inattention and relatively standard, but politically-based, unfair practices, and, more basically, his rage that, in order to support his art, he had had to compromise himself by coming into the marketplace (the setting in which Hester is first humiliated) and involve himself — "an inoffensive man of letters" — with the customs of "thick-skulled and no-hearted" men[6].

In the tension between Chillingworth and Dimmesdale, Hawthorne dramatizes the potential for worldly knowledge to adulterate the spirit. Therapeutic help and the possibility of freedom are corrupting seductions to the genuinely guilty person. The novel can be read as an allegory about an original sin (whatever happened between Hester and Arthur preceded our knowing them) and the loss of Eden in a grasping for knowledge, carnal and otherwise. It is also relentlessly, if anxiously, a psychological *tour de force*, and the emerging science of psychology can be found both between and within its lines. Etymologically, psychology is the study of the soul, the mixing of these two terms (study and soul) representing, at least potentially, exactly the kind of adulterous danger our fictional doctor and patient dramatize.

Chillingworth, and therefore Hawthorne, knew something about psychosomatic illness and about the treatment stance eventually described by psychoanalysis. "Not only the disease interested the physician, but he was strongly moved to look into the character and qualities of the patient ..." "Wherever there is a heart and an intellect, the diseases of the physical frame are tinged with peculiarities of these." In Dimmesdale, "thought and imagination were so active, and sensibility so intense, that the bodily infirmity would be likely to have its groundwork there." The doctor "strove to go deep into the patient's bosom, delving among its principles, prying into his recollections, and probing everything with a cautious touch ..."[7]

Erik Erikson once advised his trainees that "you need a history and you need a theory, then you must forget them both and let each hour stand for itself."[8] Chillingworth wanted to know his patient's history. He had theories about the unconscious interaction between mind and body. He knew about a therapeutic stance of neutrality and empathy, which might allow the unconscious to speak. "If (the investigator) possess native sagacity, and a nameless something more, — let us call it intuition; if he show no intrusive egotism, nor disagreeably prominent characteristics of his own; if he have the power . . . to bring his mind into such affinity with his patient's, that this last shall unawares have spoken what he imagines himself only to have thought; if such revelations be received without tumult, and acknowledged not so often by an uttered sympathy, as by silence, an inarticulate breath, and here and there a word, to indicate that all is understood; . . . then . . . will the soul of the sufferer . . . flow forth . . ."[9]

Belief in the soul-body connection constituted the historical foundation for treatment of mental disorders. Disease was for centuries regarded as God's punishment for sin, exorcism was used in cases of possession, and the later procedure called the "Cure of Souls" understood mysterious physical symptoms to be the result of a "pathogenic secret" (usually a sexual one) and confession to be its cure.[10] *The Scarlet Letter* takes its place within that latter tradition.

Freud stepped into and decisively introduced into this confessional tradition a scientific method. *Studies in Hysteria* in 1895 argued that the symptoms of the hysteric stemmed from a pathological secret, kept secret even from herself through the work of unconscious repression. Hypnosis, then the quasi-sleep technique of free association — with the patient in a recumbent position and the analyst not intruding into the patient's field of vision — were the methods of accessing the patient's mental life and developing the material for the interpretation of what the patient was ambivalently trying to tell both of them.

Hawthorne's knowledge of and wariness about the clinical psychology of his day were evidenced in his distress over Sophia's interest in mesmerism. From early childhood, Sophia had suffered from numerous physical ailments; her mother never expected her to marry. She became interested in the possibility of a cure for her headaches through hypnosis (also called "magnetic sleep"). Hawthorne responded with an uncharacteristic and panicky declaration: "I am unwilling that a power should be exercised on thee, of which we know neither the origin or the consequence.... Supposing that the power arises from the transfusion of one spirit into another, it seems to me that the sacredness of the individual is violated by it; there would be an intrusion into the holy of holies ... (My) view... is caused by no want of faith in mysteries; but from a deep reverence of the soul, and of the mysteries which it knows within itself."[11] Like the doctor and patient in his novel, Hawthorne linked bodily suffering and spiritual vulnerability.

Hawthorne's insight into hysterical trouble long preceded Freud, and clearly the maladies and the psychology of his day were sources of this knowledge. Another was his own life. Hawthorne's father died on a sea voyage to South America when the little boy was four. His mother (who had borne her first child seven months after her marriage) became reclusive, depressed and weakened, living out a withdrawn, though perhaps controlling, form of mourning for the rest of her life. In Sophia's ailments and weaknesses, Hawthorne found the perfect transferential life partner. He is said to have been transfixed at the first sight of her, after years of relative withdrawal in his mother's house.

He, too, was no stranger to emotionally-based ailments. Not only did he suffer periods of depression, but at age nine, following an injury to his foot, he seemed to unconsciously prolong his debilitation for over two years, using it to avoid school, to secure a place in his adopted home (his grandfather's) and to elicit a female servant's carrying him about, a form of physical affection denied to her children by his mother. The circumstances of his ailment are suggestive;[12] his grandmother had collapsed into acute grief at the near simultaneous death by stroke of her husband and the loss at sea of her son. Hawthorne may well have reacted to these events with the painful memory of his own father's death at sea, and an unconscious demand to be held might have protested the subsequent loss of his mother to depression. Hawthorne thus did not only know *about* the body's suffering with emotional trouble; he knew it first-hand in himself and, very likely, through identification with his mother.

In 1637, Hester's historical namesake, William Prynne criticized the authoritarianism of church officials and, for his crime, was branded on his cheeks with an S and an L (for Seditious Libeller).[13] Prynne claimed that the letters stood for Stigmata Laudis; he thus transformed official judgment through his own interpretation, claiming a sign connecting him, in praise, with the Lord. Dimmesdale's A can also be seen as a stigmata, an ecstatic union-in-suffering with the object of his love and his transgression. Like St. Francis, given over completely, including physically, to suffering with Christ, Dimmesdale reveals that he is *with*, in a most basic sense, Hester. He thus returns her transformational reassurance that "Thou shalt not go alone."[14]

The revelation of the scarlet letter on the flesh of Dimmesdale's chest is called the "operation of his spirit upon his body."[15] Explanations of this phenomenon included Dimmesdale's penitential self-mutilation, Chillingworth's vengeful mix of medications, and "the effect of the ever active tooth of remorse, gnawing from the inmost heart outwardly . . ."[16] In revealing it, Dimmesdale finally and publicly joins Hester, bringing her A-as-signifier together with Arthur as the signified. What Dimmesdale anticipates only as a shameful and damning admission turns out also to be a joyous reunion.

A consideration of identification illuminates not so much *what* Hawthorne knew about psychosomatic illness, but *how* he knew it. *The Scarlet Letter* powerfully suggests an answer to this question. "The scarlet letter had endowed (Hester) with a new sense . . . it gave her a *sympathetic knowledge* (my italics)of the hidden sin in other hearts."[17] It was "her passport into regions where other women dared not tread."[18] Chillingworth too has "a sympathy that will make (him) conscious"[19] though he exploits it for revenge, and Hester's daughter, Pearl, functions on purely instinctive intuition, without "a grief that should . . . humanize and make her capable of sympathy."[20] Dimmesdale, though he has "never gone through an experience" that would "lead him beyond . . . received laws,"[21] has the capacity for sympathetic knowledge even if he disavows it to his own peril. In learning of Chillingworth's betrayal, Dimmesdale says "I did know it! Was not the secret told me in the natural recoil of my heart. . . . Why did I not understand?"[22]

The answer to that question has to do with Hawthorne's romanticist mistrust of the Enlightenment exaltation of reason and with the way that illness absorbs the psyche, leading even the paranoid to fail to realize that somebody might be out to get him: "It was impossible to assign a reason for such distrust and abhorrence, so Mr. Dimmesdale, conscious that the poison of one morbid spot was infecting his heart's entire substance, attributed all his presentiments to no other cause."[23] For Hawthorne, reason deceives. In contrast, "the sympathy of Nature"[24] resonates with Hester's and Arthur's love, and "the great heart" of the people, facing Hester, Arthur and Pearl on the scaffold, "overflow(ed) with tearful sympathy, as knowing that some deep life-matter — which, if full of sin, was full of anguish and repentance likewise — was now to be laid open to them."[25]

Hawthorne always counters the polarization of good and evil — the localization, projection into and extrusion of the representation of evil being the primary effort of seemingly rational, puritanical authority — with a more complex, human, and multivalent attitude: sin *and* anguish, "fellow-sinner *and* fellow sufferer."[26] Sympathetic knowledge crosses the boundary between one person and another, and adulterates absolute judgments with the human likelihood that to truly know is to love.

If Chillingworth bears similarities, in his more benign form, to a psychoanalytically-oriented psychiatrist, Hester draws on her capacity for sympathetic knowledge to become an exceptional therapist herself. "As Hester had no selfish ends . . . people brought all their sorrows and perplexities, and besought her counsel, as one who had herself gone through a mighty trouble. Women, more especially, — in the continually recurring trials of wounded, wasted, wronged, misplaced, or erring and sinful passion, — or with the dreary burden of a heart unyielded, because unvalued and unsought, — came to Hester's cottage, demanding why they were so wretched, and what the remedy! Hester comforted and counseled them, as best she might."[27]

Hawthorne, like his three major characters, had the therapeutic gift of "heart-knowledge."[28] Dimmesdale's superiority over the rest of the church fathers has to do with his ability to speak in "the heart's native language."[29] Whether Hawthorne's gift, like Dimmesdale's, was nurtured by "the prick and anguish of his daily life"[30] is an interesting question, and one cannot help but wonder about its origins. The depth of his understanding of women and the notion of sympathetic knowledge itself would suggest that it lies in his early relationship with his mother.

On Independence Day, 1804, Nathaniel Hawthorne was born in a house on Union Street in Salem, Massachusetts. Descended from a line of public officials who tortured young women condemned as witches and later from a line of seafaring captains, Hawthorne grew up in a household of lonely, reclusive women. (In 1785, about 11 percent of the population of Salem were widows.[31] Salem paid for its commercial success by the loss of its men at sea.) There is no data about his early relationship with his mother. We do know that Hawthorne hated to be parted from her, even though she was a reserved and not particularly gratifying person. He even once expressed the wish that he had been born a girl so that he would not have to be separated from her. He also seemed to feel that she would have great difficulty in being separated from him; he was extremely frightened to tell her that he was marrying (at the age of 38), as was Sophia about making this announcement to her mother.

Most strikingly, Hawthorne reacted to his mother's death with, first of all, what his wife called a "brain fever"[32] and then with the feverish writing of *The Scarlet Letter* over a period of six months. Hawthorne described his experience at her deathbed in his journal: "I love my mother; but there has been, ever since my boyhood, a sort of coldness of intercourse between us, such as is apt to come between persons of strong feelings, if they are not managed rightly. I did not expect to be much moved at the time . . . though I knew that I should deeply remember and regret her . . . . I found tears slowly gathering in my eyes . . . for a few moments, I shook with sobs. For a long time, I knelt there, holding her hand; and surely it is the darkest hour I ever lived."[33]

Hawthorne's mother's death released him into a rare breakdown into grief, and it also released his capacity to write. We might remember here Dimmesdale's other, if minor, ailment; "his thoughts had ceased to gush"[34] in his preparation of his Election Sermon. After his encounter with Hester in the forest, "he wrote with such an impulsive flow of thought and emotion, that he fancied himself inspired."[35] Emotional reconciliation had cured a writer's block. Perhaps his mother's death had overwhelmed Hawthorne with, and freed him to express, the "strong feelings" he alluded to as dangerous "if not rightly managed." Hester listened to the Election Sermon (the date for which was determined by the Day of Resurrection) "with such intentness, and sympathized so intimately, that the sermon had throughout a meaning for her, entirely apart from its indistinguishable words."[36] As perhaps had Hawthorne's intimacy with his mother at her death; "she knew me," even if she "could only murmur a few indistinct words."[37]

———

In Freud's comment about the unfathomable place in every dream, the German word translated as the "central point" is *nabel*, the navel, the mark of the former bodily union between infant and mother. Hawthorne's capacity for identification, for sympathetic knowledge, can only have come about through early, intimate, wordless connection with his mother. It may also have been the basis for his anxiety that there could indeed be "the transfusion of one spirit into another," as though the boundaries between mother and son might be permeable and one could actually become lost in the other.

Hawthorne's father
Captain Nathaniel Hawthorne

The Scarlet Letter has been interpreted persuasively within the psychoanalytic theory of the family romance:[38] the oedipal drama of the wronged and vengeful father figure, the rivalrous and sexually guilty son and the woman over whom they struggle. It is a rich framework for meaning-making in the novel and in Hawthorne's life. A son left by his father to his mother at age four can indeed feel a kind of guilty victory, along with a fear of a vengeful return. Melville was not the only person to wonder about Hawthorne's dark secrets, and Hawthorne's comment at his mother's deathbed invites us to wonder *what* "strong feelings."

On the other hand, it could be argued that the boundary usually set by the father's forceful presence was for Hawthorne set obscurely by his absence and substantiated in his mother's apparently life-long depression. Something about her was unreachable, even if it never let go. Like Pearl relating to the scarlet letter rather than to her mother, Hawthorne as a little boy may have encountered his mother's depression as something coming between them, a pain-filled mystery to be solved, provoking longings, anger, guilt and desperate, if unconscious, curative efforts. Hester is referred to once as the "fallen mother,"[39] and during his vigil, Dimmesdale sees "his mother, turning her face away . . . methinks she might yet have thrown a pitying glance towards her son!"[40] In the climactic Revelation scene, Dimmesdale's staggers toward Hester like "the wavering effort of an infant, with its mother's arms in view . . . "[41] Hester physically supports Dimmesdale as he ascends the scaffold, an image of a mother finally holding the boy who cannot walk.

It is, however, in the story of Pearl and Hester that the mother-child relationship is most explicitly represented by Hawthorne. Like Hawthorne, Pearl is fatherless; Pearl even declares herself to "have no Heavenly Father."[42] (Chillingworth sees "no law, nor reverence for authority" in Pearl, but Dimmesdale sees "the freedom of a broken law."[43]) Pearl's innate gift is for a primitive kind of identification, including mimicry; she is instinctively attuned to Dimmesdale's reflexive gesture of putting his hand to his heart, and she *knows,* though she cannot know that she knows, that it relates to the letter on her mother's breast. "Children have . . . a sympathy in the agitations of those connected with them . . . especially, a sense of any trouble; Pearl . . . betrayed, by the very dance of her spirits, the emotions which none could detect in the marble passiveness of Hester's brow."[44] This is sympathetic knowledge in its natural, undeveloped, lived-out form.

Pearl both seeks and resists the discovery of the third party to her relationship with her mother. She relentlessly studies Dimmesdale, inquires of him, and asks for his recognition. On the other hand, the task of deciphering the scarlet letter and, of course, of understanding her mother is *hers,* her "appointed mission."[45] In the critical Brook-Side scene, Hester reconciles with Dimmesdale. Pearl, on the other side of the brook, that is, with a new boundary between herself and her mother, is felt by Hester as "estranged" from her, "out of the sphere in which she and her mother dwelt together, and . . . now vainly seeking to return to it."[46] But the truth of this had to do not with Pearl's wandering, but with Hester's having "admitted" another person, Dimmesdale, "within the circle of the mother's feelings."[47] Pearl "hardly knew where she was."[48]

Hester realizes that "Pearl misses something she has always seen me wear" (the scarlet letter which Hester has cast off). "Children will not abide any ... change in the accustomed aspect of things,"[49] says Hester, and indeed during this drama, Pearl looks again and again at her mirror image in the brook, as though to say that what is reflected back from her mother as well must be exactly the image Pearl has always known, with nothing new having come between them. When Hester takes back the scarlet letter, Pearl declares: "Now thou art my mother ... And I am thy little Pearl."[50]

It is Pearl's fate to be "humanized" by grief. The kiss from Dimmesdale she refused in the forest — the mark of her father — she embraces on the scaffold. "A spell was broken. The great scene of grief ... had developed all her sympathies; and as her tears fell upon her father's cheek, they were the pledge that she would grow up amid human joy and sorrow ... "[51] Pearl's demand (and her *appointed* mission) to be everything to her mother — in Freudian terms an oedipal insistence, from one party or the other, to admit no Third — relents and accepts with both "joy and sorrow" the Other with whom her mother has all along been in relationship. The psychoanalyst Jacques Lacan describes this as the movement from the Imaginary Order, in which only the gratifyingly mirroring twosome exists, to the Symbolic Order, which limits desire in both parties but frees a child to "grow up amid humans."[52]

The drama of *The Scarlet Letter* is, on the one hand, about separation overcome (between Arthur and Hester) and, on the other, about separation established (between Hester and Pearl). The child is, however reluctantly, freed by the mediating return of the father. Perhaps the story of Pearl, Hester and Arthur suggests a slightly different version of the oedipal triangle for Hawthorne: that at his mother's deathbed, he is released from the futile effort to cure her in order to be cured by her, and released to feel *for* her rather than simply *with* her. Perhaps Hawthorne's mother's death meant to him that she had at last joined his dead father, and that her sobbing, loving son had finally understood her lifelong absence and made his peace with it. Hawthorne had achieved the grief that had eluded him and his mother for so long. Melancholia had become mourning.

———

Hawthorne's creative gift lies in his ability to move his readers *into* his characters through identification with their most basic human emotions. This always brings about "Another View"[53] of them, beyond the initial or official one. And there is always a remainder of mystery. The power of official authority to determine meaning — the A *must* signify Adultery; Hester is *not* an individual, but a type, a symbol[54] — is continually subverted by the author's capacity to move us into sympathetic knowledge. The human subject always eludes external, fixed signification, and she does so because we feel her feelings and identify them in ourselves.

Hester's A comes to stand for Able in the townspeople's eyes (an ironic, punning reversal of the scarlet letter's being earlier referred to as the mark of Cain). It could just as easily stand for Angel, which is Dimmesdale's word for her, or for the Artist who embroiders. Like Hester, Hawthorne too is an embroiderer — of tales;[55] his A might stand for Author (a word homophonically embedded in his name, and very close in sound to the name Arthur). Hawthorne's becoming an author, in the male world he was expected to inhabit, was an ongoingly stressful act of taking authority for his life and an assertion of the gift of sympathetic knowledge he had developed in identification with a woman. In *The Scarlet Letter*, the most important A may have to do with the triumph of personal and moral Authority over institutionalized authoritarianism. A Freudian oedipal victory would have had to do with the son's *power* to defeat his father (or the official fathers of the story); oedipal resolution has to do with the surrendering of power in favor of a longer-term project of taking *authority* over one's life. This is a process of both identifying with *and* separating from parental figures, a process involving love, repudiation and grief.

———

Finally, there is Ann. "At the threshold" of the story and of the prison door is "a wild rose-bush," offering its "fragrance and fragile beauty . . . that the deep heart of Nature could pity and be kind . . . " "It had sprung up under the footsteps of the sainted Ann Hutchinson,"[56] a historical figure and leader of the Antinomians who believed that "the law is fulfilled in love"[57] and that God spoke directly to the justified soul, without the necessary mediation of the official (male) ministry. Governor Winthrop, upon whose death the townspeople interpret the A in the sky as referring to his Angelic status, once angrily declared to Ann Hutchinson: "We are your judges, not you ours . . . "[58]

Banished from the soil of Boston in 1638, Ann nevertheless gives birth to a rose bush in Hawthorne's tale. This notion of fertile, female soil contrasts with Dimmesdale's worries that grass would never grow on his grave, and with the description of Chillingworth as potentially "sink(ing) into the earth, leaving a barren and blasted spot." Hawthorne had himself had a dream, years before, of lying down to sleep and awakening to find the earth completely burned beneath him.[59] But there is "an absolute circle of radiance"[60] on the floor around Pearl and "a magic circle"[61] around Hester. Hawthorne seems to be highlighting the generative and emotional integrity of women in contrast to the sterilizing officiousness and guilty compromises of men, including himself.

Ann Hutchinson's drama of judgment is also Hester's. Pearl is the blossom of both. Pearl "cr(ies) for a red rose";[62] she is even named "Red Rose"[63] by one of the ministers. After *The Scarlet Letter*, Hawthorne and Sophia had one more child. Rose grew up to become a nun ministering to cancer patients. She took the name Mother Alphonsa — alpha, the Greek letter A. For Hester, Pearl is "the scarlet letter endowed with life."[64] Can we discern in the story of Rose — in her life's work, in her assumed name — the playing out of an unconscious sympathetic knowledge between herself and her father, and the carrying forward, as though his naming her had "endowed" it "with life," the vital mission of transforming an A?

---

[1] James R. Mellow, *Nathaniel Hawthorne in His Times*, (Baltimore and London: The Johns Hopkins University Press, 1980).

[2] Edwin Haviland Miller, *Salem Is My Dwelling Place*, (Iowa City: University of Iowa Press, 1991), 9.

[3] Nathaniel Hawthorne, *The Scarlet Letter*, (Oxford and New York: Oxford University Press, 1990), 119.

[4] Hawthorne, 123.

[5] Ibid.

[6] Ken Egan, Jr., "The adulteress in the marketplace: Hawthorne and *The Scarlet Letter*", Studies in the Novel, 1995, 27:5.

[7] Hawthorne, 123-124.

[8] Personal communication.

[9] Hawthorne, 124.

[10] Henri F.Ellenberger, *The Discovery of the Unconscious*, (New York: Basic Books, Inc., 1970).

[11] Mellow, 190.

[12] Miller, 48.

[13] Brian Harding, "Introduction" to Nathaniel Hawthorne, *The Scarlet Letter*, (Oxford and New York: Oxford University Press, 1990), vii-viii.

[14] Hawthorne, 198.

[15] Hawthorne, 258.

16 Ibid.
17 Hawthorne, 86.
18 Hawthorne, 199.
19 Hawthorne, 75.
20 Hawthorne, 184.
21 Hawthorne, 200.
22 Hawthorne, 194.
23 Hawthorne, 140.
24 Hawthorne, 203.
25 Hawthorne, 254.
26 Hawthorne, 67.
27 Hawthorne, 263.
28 Hawthorne, 260.
29 Hawthorne, 142.
30 Hawthorne, 141.
31 Miller, 11.
32 Miller, 273.
33 Mellow, 297.
34 Hawthorne, 223.
35 Hawthorne, 225.
36 Hawthorne, 243.
37 Mellow,297.
38 Elmer Kennedy-Andrews, ed.,
   *Nathaniel Hawthorne: The Scarlet
   Letter*, (New York: Columbia
   University Press, 1999).
39 Hawthorne, 117.

40 Hawthorne, 145.
41 Hawthorne, 251.
42 Hawthorne, 98.
43 Hawthorne, 134.
44 Hawthorne, 228.
45 Hawthorne, 180.
46 Hawthorne, 208.
47 Ibid.
48 Ibid.
49 Hawthorne, 210.
50 Hawthorne, 211.
51 Hawthorne, 256.
52 Jacques Lacan, Ecrits, (New York:
   W. W. Norton, 1977).
53 Hawthorne, 159.
54 Harding, xx.
55 Harding, xxxvi
56 Hawthorne, 48.
57 Hawthorne, 274.
58 Harding, xvii.
59 Mellow, 308.
60 Hawthorne, 90.
61 Hawthorne, 234.
62 Hawthorne, 107.
63 Hawthorne, 110.
64 Hawthorne, 102.

Dido's Curse:
Hawthorne's
Unwilling Radicalism

By Michael T. Gilmore

Thoreau famously brought Homer's *Iliad* with him to Walden Pond, and he was fond of quoting Ossian, but Hawthorne's favorite epic poet was Virgil, and he would probably have chosen *The Aeneid* as his favorite classical work. This small detail holds a world of meaning. It encapsulates the difference between one antebellum writer, Thoreau, who opposed the state, and another, Hawthorne, who embraced its imperial destiny and championed the status quo. Ossian was the voice of a lost cause, Scottish nationalism, and Homer made a comeback during the romantic age because he seemed a kind of naïf, singing of tribal chieftains and primitive warfare. Virgil, on the other hand, allied himself with the ideology of empire. He was the unabashed apologist for Augustus and the dominance of Rome.

The Virgil/Hawthorne connection might seem no more than a footnote to what has now become a familiar picture of the Salem novelist. It adds a literary patina to his well-known sycophancy to power and distaste for radical ideas. Hawthorne, let us recall, played Virgilian publicist to his own third-rate Augustus, Franklin Pierce, whose hagiographic campaign biography he compiled in exchange for a government sinecure. Hawthorne defended compromise and deferral of action on slavery, and in his fiction he allows no disruptive character to escape his chastening. He clips the wings of his subversive heroine, Hester Prynne, marries the dissenter Holgrave to the conventional Phoebe Pyncheon, and kills off the feminist Zenobia. He gave his greatest novel, *The Scarlet Letter*, an epic form of twenty-four chapters, as if to acknowledge his own role as cheerleader for the American imperium.

The trouble with this picture is that it ignores Hawthorne's ambivalence; or, better yet, his unwilling stake in the radicalism he abhorred. And here his attachment to *The Aeneid* introduces an unexpected complication. Eighteenth- and nineteenth-century admirers of Virgil's masterpiece did not always find its establishment politics to their liking. Quite as often, they cherished the poem's portrayal of the Carthaginian queen, Dido, who takes Aeneas as her lover and is then abandoned by the Trojan when he rededicates himself to his high mission of founding Rome. Dido does not submit uncomplainingly to her rejection. She sends off her faithless suitor with a curse, vowing that she will be avenged:

.... *Then, though absent, I*
shall hunt you down with blackened firebrands;
and when chill death divides my soul and body,
a Shade, I shall be present everywhere.

This episode, which is told in Book IV of *The Aeneid*, spawned a host of interpretations, the most influential of which paid tribute to Dido as a figure for the victimized but unpacified other, defiant even in defeat. The English composer Henry Purcell devoted his single opera to *Dido and Aeneas* (1689), and the father of psychoanalysis, Sigmund Freud, saw in the fiery queen's curse an omen of Semitic retribution against imperial power.

Hawthorne's work abounds in prophecies and curses. The two-speech acts, if not quite interchangeable, share a common premise of language's agency. They are utterances that bring about results. Hawthorne tends to put these speeches in the mouths of characters who are otherwise vanquished by history. Their words are variations on Dido's curse, promises that the proscribed positions they represent — anti-patriarchalism, class resentment, the power of individual conscience against orthodoxy — will prevail at some later date. Hawthorne simultaneously rules those dissident allegiances out of bounds and gives them the final say in his narratives. The pattern amounts to a half-smothered protest against his own conservatism, and it is nowhere more apparent than in *The Blithedale Romance*, the novel he published in the same year, 1852, that he offered his Virgilian hymn to *The Life of Franklin Pierce*.

Hawthorne's dual impulses first emerge in *The Scarlet Letter* (1850), his inaugural American romance, the book that appropriately serves up two prophesies in its concluding chapters. The initial one by Dimmesdale has nothing but applause for the American experiment, whereas the second by Hester shows faint but ominous signs of mutating into something threatening. According to Hawthorne, Dimmesdale's Election Day Sermon, delivered just minutes before his confession and death on the scaffold, departs from Old Testament prophecy in that it does not decree "judgments and ruin" on his country. On the contrary, the minister foretells "a high and glorious destiny for the newly gathered people of the Lord."

A few pages later, the mood of euphoria yields to Hester's far more ambiguous revelation. The heroine has returned from her years abroad with Pearl to settle permanently in New England, and her cottage becomes a gathering place for all those suffering from the injustices of patriarchal society (much as Hester herself suffered at the hands of the Puritan elders). She confides her own "truth" to these unhappy women, assuring them of a "brighter period" when gender relations will be established "on a surer ground of mutual happiness." Dimmesdale's vision of the future has arguably been realized in the expanding American republic; Hester's definitely has not, if we can put any faith in the angry outbursts of her nineteenth-century successor, Zenobia, who constantly rails against male oppression. (Or if we read the Declaration of Sentiments issued by the women's rights convention at Seneca Falls in 1848.) Were Hester able to check on the fate of her prediction, one could easily imagine her words assuming an angry edge and devolving into a curse.

The darkening of prophetic utterance moves to center stage in *The House of the Seven Gables* (1851), where a poor but proud family, the Maules, are dispossessed of their homestead and retaliate through language. Wrongly convicted of witchcraft, Matthew Maule pronounces a Dido-like curse against his persecutor, the powerful Colonel Pyncheon:

"God will give him blood to drink!" This sentence comes to pass on the
very day that the newly built mansion is consecrated, and the Colonel is
discovered dead in his chair, his beard and ruff soaked in blood. Moreover, the potency of the oath persists all the way into the nineteenth
century, lending verbal authority to the "lawless" Holgrave, the
daguerreotypist, storywriter, and reformer who is actually a Maule.

Holgrave recites one of his narratives, "Alice Pyncheon," to the utterly
ordinary Phoebe; the telling gives him momentary dominion over his
auditor. But the hero, in what Hawthorne clearly intended to be a renun-
ciation of speech's transgressive energy, abjures mastery over the girl, and
he later goes on to disclaim his radicalism in a declaration of love.
Although we are supposed to believe that marriage and maturation have
dispelled the specter of unconciliated rage, the text, once again, puts up
resistance to its own spirit of accommodation. Holgrave finds the resolve
to speak his proposal only because Judge Jaffrey Pyncheon, the persecutor of Clifford, has met his death in a replay of the past. Choking on his
own blood, this latter-day avatar of the Colonel is felled by Maule's curse.
And the sentimentalism of the novel's conclusion is quietly but firmly
qualified by a last nod to illicit discourse: the Pyncheon elm whispers
"unintelligible prophecies" as the lovers drive off into the sunset.

Hawthorne's fictionalized account of Brook Farm brings to a climax
his fascination with outsider speech. Indeed, in this work the Virgilian
prototype sheds its disguises and steps forward as the catalyst of the plot.
Coverdale's story of Blithedale is nominally a chronicle of failure. The
utopian community self-destructs, Hollingsworth and Zenobia are
rendered harmless, and the poet-narrator, disaffected by his fling at
idealism, abandons all faith in societal reform. The text's neo-
conservative message could not be more straightforward: dreams of
betterment produce more ill than good. The wise learn to accept things
as they are.

But capitulating to the existing state of affairs cannot banish verbal
insurrection, with its pledge of revenge for the defeated. The regal Zenobia
has fallen for a man who, like Aeneas, appears to return her affection but
in actuality cares only for his exalted destiny, in this case the project of
reforming criminals. Like the Carthaginian ruler, Zenobia has been
married before and humiliates herself in this second love; and she too
has a sibling who figures prominently in the denouement. When

Hollingsworth eventually jilts the heroine for her sister Priscilla, Zenobia refuses to acquiesce in her betrayal. She lets loose with a malediction that paraphrases Dido's: "Tell him he has murdered me!" she shrieks at Coverdale. "Tell him that I'll haunt him!"

The curse comes true: haunt her false-hearted paramour she does. But before then we get the chapter in which Zenobia, still reprising her model in Virgil, takes her own life in histrionic fashion. The setting for both suicides is "Night," while the world sleeps (*Aeneid*, IV, 723). Dido falls on her lover's sword and three times struggles to rise before expiring; Zenobia drowns herself, and her corpse is dragged from the water with an iron hook, hands clenched and knees bent in showy prayer. In an even closer echo of her predecessor's manner of death, Hawthorne's heroine has also suffered a disfiguring sword wound: the hook, which is wielded by Hollingsworth, pierces her breast. This ghastly outcome will not leave the prison reformer in peace. Confronted a year later, he confesses that he has been occupied with a single criminal, himself. Coverdale claims that he can almost see the "vindictive shadow" of Zenobia dogging Hollingsworth's side.

A dramatic utterance that disturbs the triumph of conservatism: each of Hawthorne's romances incorporates a fictional facsimile of the discursive turmoil of his culture. It is not enough to attribute these eruptions to unresolved feelings about feminism or economic injustice or utopian blueprints. The verbal trespasses have deeper roots in what came to be known as the slave power conspiracy to extinguish freedom of speech. Hawthorne wrote at a time when the slaveholding class wanted no debate about the peculiar institution in the public forums. Stifle antislavery agitation, Southern fire-eaters warned the North, or they would withdraw from the Union. Hawthorne the trimmer agreed with these enemies of open discussion, as we know from his efforts on behalf of the doughface Pierce. But his art would not assent without a protest. "Dido's curse" is the proof that this proponent of compromise was strongly stirred by compromise's opposite. As a supporter of appeasing the South, Hawthorne may have welcomed the attempted ban on contentiousness, but as an author, he could never forget that, like the abolitionists he disapproved of, he owed his influence to the untamed authority of language.

Pamela Dalton's interpretation of the gilded eagle atop the Salem Custom House seems to have been inspired by Hawthorne's "Introduction to The Scarlet Letter" written after losing his position in that very building: "Many people are seeking, at this very moment, to shelter themselves under the wing of the federal eagle; imagining, I presume, that her bosom has all the softness and snugness of an eider-down pillow. But she has no great tenderness, even in her best moods, and, sooner or later, — oftener soon than late, — is apt to fling off her nestlings with a scratch of her claw, a dab of her beak, or a rankling wound from her barbed arrows."

A Heap of Broken Fragments: Hawthorne and Politics

By Brenda Wineapple

In 1879, Henry James published a book in the *English Man of Letters* series about Nathaniel Hawthorne, whose death fifteen years earlier had moved him to tears. Now, in *Hawthorne*, James was able to celebrate his literary forefather as an original genius with a cat-like faculty of seeing in the dark — although James also noted, more than once, that very little was very dark in Hawthorne's America.

As one might suspect, the book is as much about the sunny cultural wasteland James had sought to escape as it is about Nathaniel Hawthorne. For to James, America, provincial and crude, is a place without sovereign, court, personal loyalty, aristocracy, church, clergy, diplomatic service, country gentlemen, palaces, castles, manors, country-houses, parsonages, thatched cottages, ivied ruins, cathedrals, abbeys, little Norman churches, great universities, public schools, literature, novels, museums, pictures, political society and sporting class. The list is James's. So is the sardonic conclusion. "If these things are left out, everything is left out."

America, where actualities are the *sine qua non* of existence, is no place for an artist. Its atmosphere is too thin, its soil too light to produce great writers. Yet to James Hawthorne's America also represents the good old days of what, today, we call American "exceptionalism." Born into a spanking new century (the nineteenth), men like Hawthorne breathed deep the brisk air of freedom and hope and easy-going prosperity (a few nasty Panics and recessions notwithstanding) "that implanted," according to James, "a kind of superstitious faith in the grandeur of the country, its duration, its immunity from the usual troubles of earthly empires." The future looked clear, happy and bright — if one excludes, of course, the annoying shadow cast by the "peculiar institution" (the phrase is now Hawthorne's) of slavery.

Soon the pretty illusions were destroyed by war, when America's best and brightest marched off to the slaughter that muddied the soil with blood. Fratricidal death in such genial, sunshiny country? It couldn't happen. Yet it had. "Nothing was left for them but to hang their heads and close their eyes," wrote James of Hawthorne's generation; or, in the case of Hawthorne himself, to die of disillusion.

To James, then, Hawthorne was an addled innocent, somewhat benighted, burdened with genius he doesn't quite understand. As for his political perspicacity, it's moot. Hawthorne is a precocious writer almost in spite of himself, or at least in spite of his country, a romancer finally more comfortable in the seventeenth century than his own, a recluse who walks abroad only at night and scurries for cover whenever well-meaning neighbors come to call. Moreover, he's an old-fashioned Democrat with an appetite for the commoner stuff and the plainer people, faithful to his party (despite its pro-slavery wing) and his friends (despite their pro-slavery views), and exempt from worldly preoccupations and "vulgar efforts" (whatever they are).

But Nathaniel Hawthorne was not an American rube, wide-eyed at malfeasance and heedless of current events. Not at all. Nor was he oblivious to the women and men reshaping his world: Margaret Fuller, William Lloyd Garrison, Abraham Lincoln, Charles Sumner, as well as Emerson, Longfellow, Alcott, Douglass, and John Brown. They were his contemporaries, who sprang from the same thin soil that he did. And he too tilled that soil, after his own fashion.

In 1841, for instance, a hoe slung over a shoulder, Hawthorne plunked down a hard-earned one thousand dollars to become a charter-member of the Brook Farm commune, and even if his short-lived attendance there seems out of step with his sulky individualism, Hawthorne very much wanted to believe in the democratic ideal trumpeted by his friend John Louis O'Sullivan, editor of the premier literary and political journal, *United States Magazine and Democratic Review*. The object of democracy, O'Sullivan wrote in the stirring first issue, "is to emancipate the mind of the mass of men from the degrading, & disenheartening fetters of social distinctions & advantages; to bid it walk abroad through the free creation 'in its own majesty,' to war against all fraud, oppression, & violence, by striking at their root, to reform all the infinitely varied human misery which has grown out of the old & false ideas by which the world has been so long misgoverned."

This does not mean Hawthorne's politics — like his writing — are warm, fuzzy, or socially acceptable. Far from it. The Democrats themselves were not the New England establishment party, nor were they the party of Emerson or even of John Greenleaf Whittier, an abolitionist; rather, they stood for Jackson, expansionism, an indigenous literature, an implicit agrarianism, copyright reform, nationalism, optimism, states' rights, and, ultimately, slavery. Hawthorne joined their number, in spite of his quizzical cast of mind and his doubts about human goodness. "Perhaps your faith in the idea is deeper than you are aware," an O'Sullivanish character in one of his early stories responds to him. "You are at least a Democrat; and methinks no scanty share of such faith is essential to the adoption of that creed."

Yes, Hawthorne wanted to believe, and if he couldn't quite get his arms around a perfectible human nature, he was no advocate of the status quo — or the capitalists, industrialists and self-styled aristocrats. In fact, for nine years, from 1837-1846, he published regularly in the exuberant *Democratic Review* until O'Sullivan left, offering it some of his best stories, like "Rappaccini's Daughter," as well as the satires like "The Celestial Railroad," "The Procession of Life," or "The New Adam and Eve," in which he wonders "why one portion of earth's lost inhabitants was rolling in luxury, while the multitude was toiling for scanty food?"

Though progressively disaffected from the body politic as he grew older, Hawthorne consistently wrote political novels in the largest sense of the term, with the possible exception of his first, *Fanshawe* (a novel of vocation). The body politic is real and palpable in *The Scarlet Letter*, where beetle-browed Puritans wield a theocracy that doesn't quite — can't, in fact — extinguish personal desire. *The House of the Seven Gables*, drawing on similar resources, is a novel about the not-so hidden injuries of class in an America where, writes Hawthorne, "somebody is always at the drowning-point. The tragedy is enacted with as continual a repetition as that of a popular drama on a holiday, and, nevertheless, is felt as deeply, perhaps, as when an hereditary noble sinks below his order. More deeply; since, with us, rank is the grosser substance of wealth and a splendid establishment, and has not spiritual existence after the death of these, but dies hopelessly along with them."

Then there's *The Blithedale Romance* in which Hawthorne undoes his own youthful commitment to Brook Farm while excoriating the community's muddled utopianism. "It struck me as rather odd," Hawthorne's narrator comments, "that one of the first questions raised, after our separation from the greedy, struggling, self-seeking world, should relate to the possibility of getting the advantage over the outside barbarians, in their own field of labor. But, to own the truth, I very soon became sensible, that, as regarded society at large, we stood in a position of new hostility, rather than new brotherhood."

To the extent that the tone of this novel is mordant, Hawthorne's next production — his campaign biography of Franklin Pierce — makes cynical sense. The dream of a new world a thing of the past, he was angling for another political appointment; he'd already worked in the Boston and Salem Custom House and was ignominiously fired from the latter post when the Whigs took over in 1848. A presidential race loomed in 1852 with spoils aplenty for him, should Pierce win. But Hawthorne's commitment to Pierce was not simple opportunism.

A close friend since their college days, Hawthorne considered Pierce a fit man for the job, or at least as fit as anyone eager for it, and certainly not one to toady to the abolitionists, whom Hawthorne and Pierce both loathed. "When a good man has long devoted himself to a particular kind of beneficence — to one species of reform," Hawthorne scoffed in the pages of the *Democratic Review*, "he is apt to become narrowed into the limits of the path wherein he treads, and to fancy that there is no other good to be done on earth but that self-same good to which he has put his hand, and in the very mode that best suits his own conceptions. All else is worthless."

While Hawthorne objected to the odious Fugitive Slave Law, he supported the Compromise of 1850, and he continued to consider all abolitionists, both radical and political ones, as dangerous reformers. As for slavery, he remarked in *The Life of Franklin Pierce* that he admired Pierce for never shunning "the obloquy that sometimes threatened to pursue the northern man, who dared to love that great and sacred reality — his whole, united, native country — better than the mistiness of a philanthropic theory." Slaves be damned; or, more to the point, "antislavery agitation" be damned. Only the Constitution counts. "Merely human wisdom and human efforts cannot subvert it [slavery], except by tearing to pieces the Constitution, breaking the pledges which it sanctions, and severing into distracted fragments that common country, which Providence brought into one nation."

Franklin Pierce

Supporting Pierce, Hawthorne defines slavery as "one of those evils, which Divine Providence does not leave to be remedied by human contrivances, but which, in its own good time, by some means impossible to be anticipated, but of the simplest and easiest operation, when all its uses shall have been fulfilled, it causes to vanish like a dream. There is no instance," he continues, "in all history, of the human will and intellect having perfected any great moral reform by methods which it adapted to that end; but the progress of the world, at every stop, leaves some evil or wrong on the path behind it, which the wisest of mankind, of their own set purpose, could never have found the way to rectify."

Disturbing as it might be, Hawthorne's despair-drenched passivity lies at the root of his artistry. In other words, Hawthorne embeds his tragic vision — that our ends seldom match our aims — in a prose that rings with the ironies of human expectation disappointed, again and again, by human history. This is the subject of his last published novel, *The Marble Faun*, set in Rome, a city redolent of history's broken fragments — chipped statues, cracked columns — each of which speaks eloquently of time and decay and vain but cherished hope: "You look through a vista of century beyond century — through much shadow, and a little sunshine — through barbarism and civilization, alternating with one another, like actors that have pre-arranged their parts — through a broad pathway of progressive generations, bordered by palaces and temples, and bestridden by old, triumphal arches, until, in the distance, you behold the obelisks, with their unintelligible inscriptions, hinting at a Past infinitely more remote than history can define. Your own life is as nothing, when compared with that immeasurable distance; but still you demand, none the less earnestly, a gleam of sunshine, instead of a speck of shadow, on the stop or two that will bring you to your quiet rest."

Politicians take the short view, and so they should: emancipation now, peace now. Novelists take a longer view. And for a searching writer like Hawthorne, the long view stretches out to a grim horizon that simultaneously entices and appalls, as Emily Dickinson once noted, with beauty and crushing cruelty (a source, not coincidentally, of Hawthorne's wit and humor). A consummate stylist, Hawthorne delineates that dark horizon in graceful sentences that, themselves, reveal for a moment the best that humans can do. "The beautiful Idea at once asserted its immortality, and converted that heap of forlorn fragments into a whole, as perfect to the mind, if not to the eye, as when the new marble gleamed with snowy lustre." As he wrote elsewhere, life is made of marble and mud.

Hawthorne was not caught unprepared for war. But he utterly detested it. A skeptic about organized religion, progressive history, human endeavor, emancipation — in fact, about everything — Hawthorne considered war nothing more than high-class butchery. And in portraying society as fallen — and racist — as himself, he points out a central, if not absurd, paradox, as he sees it, of the bloodbath: "Whosoever may be benefited by the result of this war," he writes in "Chiefly About War Matters," "it will not be the present generation of negroes, the childhood of whose race is now gone forever, and who must henceforth fight a hard battle with the world, on very unequal terms."

These unequal terms are his point. America is fallen precisely because of the hypocrisy that, in one form or another, perpetually is Hawthorne's subject, whether he is writing about Puritans, Tories, transcendentalists, Brook Farmers, or abolitionists. That is, America is conceived in freedom and slavery, and with this insight, Hawthorne moves beyond a consideration of local politics, beyond even his own racism (to the extent it's possible) to a searing perception of America writ large. The slaves "are our brethren," he writes, "as being lineal descendants from the Mayflower, the fated womb of which, in her first voyage, sent forth a brood of Pilgrims upon Plymouth Rock, and, in a subsequent one, spawned Slaves upon the southern soil: — a monstrous birth, but with which we have an instinctive sense of kindred."

Hawthorne hated the world as he found it; he did what he could to change it in the way, as O'Sullivan once hoped, that literature might transform it, and yet he was too honest to pretend that he could, or that if he could, that what he wrought was necessarily or inevitably for the good, or that its goodness or elegance might last. Still, he was very much a man of his time, not above it, who captured this era in political homilies and enigmatic tales, the source and strength of which are social and psychological, a bit of both and a bit of neither, in that they confront the same basic unfairness that politics — and then war — intends, or pretends, to fix.

That is, Hawthorne's is an ontological response to the world during an era when such a response seems beside the point at best, cruelly insensitive at worst. Such may be his desperate shortcoming as a human being, but it forms him as a writer. There are no blandishments in Hawthorne's world, no easy answers, no final escape from the slow erosion of time or from despair and human folly. Hester Prynne, Young Goodman Brown, Wakefield, and the minister who wears a creepy black veil: his characters endure because Hawthorne identifies with those who are defeated or bewildered or have nowhere to go precisely because a world of certainty (or, better yet, some misty fantasy of it, likes James') dissolves into a heap of broken fragments right before our eyes.

Chiefly about War Matters by a Peaceable Man

By Nathaniel Hawthorne

[This article appeared in the Atlantic Monthly *for July 1862, and is now first reprinted among Hawthorne's collected writings. The editor of the magazine objected to sundry paragraphs in the manuscript, and these were cancelled with the consent of the author, who himself supplied all the footnotes that accompanied the article when it was published. It has seemed best to retain them in the present reproduction. One of the suppressed passages, in which President Lincoln is described, has since been printed, and is therefore restored to its proper place in the following pages. — G. P. L., 1883, Riverside Edition]*

[Editor's note: G.P.L. is George Parsons Lathrop, Hawthorne's son-in-law, who edited the Houghton Mifflin Riverside Press editions of the 1880s.]

There is no remoteness of life and thought, no hermetically sealed seclusion, except, possibly, that of the grave, into which the disturbing influences of this war do not penetrate. Of course, the general heart-quake of the country long ago knocked at my cottage-door, and compelled me, reluctantly, to suspend the contemplation of certain fantasies, to which, according to my harmless custom, I was endeavoring to give a sufficiently life-like aspect to admit of their figuring in a romance. As I make no pretensions to state-craft or soldiership, and could promote the common weal neither by valor nor counsel, it seemed, at first, a pity that I should be debarred from such unsubstantial business as I had contrived for myself, since nothing more genuine was to be substituted for it. But I magnanimously considered that there is a kind of treason in insulating one's self from the universal fear and sorrow, and thinking one's idle thoughts in the dread time of civil war; and could a man be so cold and hard-hearted he would better deserve to be sent to Fort Warren than many who have found their way thither on the score of violent, but misdirected sympathies. I remembered the touching rebuke administered by King Charles to that rural squire the echo of whose hunting-horn came to the poor monarch's ear on the morning before a battle, where the sovereignty and constitution of England were to be set at a stake. So I gave myself up to reading newspapers and listening to the click of the telegraph, like other people; until, after a great many months of such pastime, it grew so abominably irksome that I determined to look a little more closely at matters with my own eyes.

Accordingly we set out — a friend and myself — towards Washington, while it was still the long, dreary January of our Northern year, though March in name; nor were we unwilling to clip a little margin off the five months' winter, during which there is nothing genial in New England save the fireside. It was a clear, frosty morning, when we started. The sun shone brightly on snow-covered hills in the neighborhood of Boston, and burnished the surface of frozen ponds; and the wintry weather kept along with us while we trundled through Worcester and Springfield, and all those old, familiar towns, and through the village-cities of Connecticut. In New York the streets were afloat with liquid mud and slosh. Over New Jersey there was still a thin covering of snow, with the face of Nature visible through the rents in her white shroud, though with little or no symptom of reviving life. But when we reached Philadelphia, the air was mild and balmy; there was but a patch or two of dingy winter here and there, and the bare, brown fields about the city were ready to be green. We had met the Spring half-way, in her slow progress from the South; and if we kept onward at the same pace, and could get through the Rebel lines, we should soon come to fresh grass, fruit-blossoms, green peas, strawberries, and all such delights of early summer.

On our way, we heard many rumors of the war, but saw few signs of it. The people were staid and decorous, according to their ordinary fashion; and business seemed about as brisk as usual, — though, I suppose, it was considerably diverted from its customary channels into warlike ones. In the cities, especially in New York, there was a rather prominent display of military goods at the shop windows, — such as swords with gilded scabbards and trappings, epaulets, carbines, revolvers, and sometimes a great iron cannon at the edge of the pavement, as if Mars had dropped one of his pocket-pistols there, while hurrying to the field. As railway-companions, we had now and then a volunteer in his French-gray great-coat, returning from furlough, or a new-made officer traveling to join his regiment, in his new-made uniform, which was perhaps all of the military character that he had about him, — but proud of his eagle-buttons, and likely enough to do them honor before the gilt should be wholly dimmed. The country, in short, so far as bustle and movement went, was more quiet than in ordinary times, because so large a proportion of its restless elements had been drawn towards the seat of the conflict. But the air was full of a vague disturbance. To me, at least, it seemed so, emerging from such a solitude as has been hinted at, and the more impressible by rumors and indefinable presentiments, since I had not lived, like other men, in an atmosphere of continual talk about the war. A battle was momentarily expected on the Potomac; for, though our army was still on the hither side of the river, all of us were looking towards the mysterious and terrible Manassas, with the idea that somewhere in its neighborhood lay a ghastly battlefield, yet to be fought, but foredoomed of old to be bloodier than the one where we had reaped such shame. Of all haunted places, methinks such a destined field should be thickest thronged with ugly phantoms, ominous of mischief through ages beforehand.

Beyond Philadelphia there was a much greater abundance of military people. Between Baltimore and Washington a guard seemed to hold every station along the railroad; and frequently, on the hill-sides, we saw a collection of weather-beaten tents, the peaks of which, blackened with smoke, indicated that they had been made comfortable by stove-heat throughout the winter. At several commanding positions we saw fortifications, with the muzzles of cannon protruding from the ramparts, the slopes of which were made of the yellow earth of that region, and still unsodded;

whereas, till these troublous times, there have been no forts but what were grass-grown with the lapse of at least a lifetime of peace. Our stopping-places were thronged with soldiers, some of whom came through the cars asking for newspapers that contained accounts of the battle between the Merrimack and Monitor, which had been fought the day before. A railway-train met us, conveying a regiment out of Washington to some unknown point; and reaching the capital, we filed out of the station between lines of soldiers, who have heretofore founded their claims to public regard; but it behooves civilians to consider their wretched prospects in the future, and assume the military button before it is too late.

We were not in time to see Washington as a camp. On the very day of our arrival sixty thousand men had crossed the Potomac on their march towards Manassas; and almost with their first step into the Virginia mud, the phantasmagory of a countless host and impregnable ramparts, before which they had so long remained quiescent, dissolved quite away. It was as if General McClellan had thrust his sword into a gigantic enemy, and, beholding him suddenly collapse, had discovered to himself and the world that he had merely punctured an enormously swollen bladder. There are instances of a similar character in old romances, where great armies are long kept at bay by the arts of necromancers, who build airy towers and battlements, and muster warriors of terrible aspect, and thus feign a defence of seeming impregnability, until some bolder champion of the besiegers' dashes forward to try an encounter with the foremost foeman, and finds him melt away in the death-grapple. With such heroic adventures let the march upon Manassas be hereafter reckoned. The whole business, though connected with the destinies of a nation, takes inevitably a tinge of the ludicrous. The vast preparation of men and warlike material, — the majestic patience and docility with which the people waited through those weary and dreary months, — the martial skill, courage, and caution, with which our movement was ultimately made, — and, at last, the tremendous shock with which we were brought suddenly up against nothing at all! The Southerners show little sense of humor nowadays, but I think they must have meant to provoke a laugh at our expense, when they planted those Quaker guns. At all events, no other Rebel artillery has played upon us with such overwhelming effect.

The troops being gone, we had the better leisure and opportunity to look into other matters. It is natural enough to suppose that the centre and heart of Washington is the Capitol; and certainly, in its outward aspect, the world has not many statelier or more beautiful edifices, nor any, I should suppose, more skillfully adapted to legislative purposes, and to all accompanying needs. But, etc., etc. [1]

[1] *We omit several paragraphs here, in which the author speaks of some prominent Members of Congress with a freedom that seems to have been not unkindly meant, but might be liable to mis-construction. As he admits that he never listened to an important debate, we can hardly recognize his qualifications to estimate these gentlemen, in their legislative and oratorical capacities.*

We found one man, however, at the Capitol, who was satisfactorily adequate to the business which brought him thither. In quest of him, we went through halls, galleries, and corridors, and ascended a noble stair-case, balustraded with a dark and beautifully variegated marble from Tennessee, the richness of which is quite a sufficient cause for objecting to the secession of that State. At last we came to a barrier of pine boards, built right across the stairs. Knocking at a rough, temporary door, we thrust a card beneath; and in a minute or two it was opened by a person in his shirt-sleeves, a middle-aged figure, neither tall nor short, of Teutonic build and aspect, with an ample beard of a ruddy tinge and chestnut hair. He looked at us, in the first place, with keen and somewhat guarded eyes, as if it were not his practice to vouchsafe any great warmth of greeting, except upon sure ground of observation. Soon, however, his look grew kindly and genial (not that it had ever been in the least degree repulsive, but only reserved), and Leutze allowed us to gaze at the car-toon of his great fresco, and talked about it unaffectedly, as only a man of true genius can speak of his own works. Meanwhile, the noble design spoke for itself upon the wall. A sketch in color, which we saw afterwards, helped us to form some distant and flickering notion of what the picture will be, a few months hence, when these bare outlines, already so rich in thought and suggestiveness, shall glow with a fire of their own, — a fire which, I truly believe, will consume every other pictorial decoration of the Capitol, or, at least, will compel us to banish those stiff and respect-able productions to some less conspicuous gallery. The work will be emphatically original and American, embracing characteristics that neither art nor literature have yet dealt with, and producing new forms of artistic beauty from the natural features of the Rocky-Mountain region, which Leutze seems to have studied broadly and minutely. The garb of the hunters and wanderers of those deserts, too, under his free and natural management is shown as the most picturesque of costumes. But it would be doing this admirable painter no kind office to overlay his picture with any more of my colorless and uncertain words; so I shall merely add that it looked full of energy, hope, progress, irrepressible movement onward, all represented in a momentary pause of triumph; and it was most cheering to feel its good augury at this dismal time, when our country might seem to have arrived at such a deadly stand-still.

It was an absolute comfort, indeed, to find Leutze so quietly busy at this great national work, which is destined to glow for centuries on the walls of the Capitol, if that edifice shall stand, or must share its fate, if treason shall succeed in subverting it with the Union which it represents. It was delightful to see him so calmly elaborating his design, while other men doubted and feared, or hoped treacherously, and whispered to one another that the nation would exist only a little longer, or that, if a remnant still held together, its centre and seat of government would be far northward and westward of Washington. But the artist keeps right on, firm of heart and hand, drawing his outlines with an unwavering pencil, beautifying and idealizing our rude, material life, and thus manifesting that we have an indefeasible claim to a more enduring national existence. In honest truth, what with the hope-inspiring influence of the design, and what with Leutze's undisturbed evolvement of it, I was exceedingly encouraged, and allowed these cheerful auguries to weigh against a sinister omen that was pointed out to me in another part of the Capitol. The freestone walls of the central edifice are pervaded with great cracks, and threaten to come thundering down, under the immense weight of the iron dome, — an appropriate catastrophe enough, if it should occur on the day when we drop the Southern stars out of our flag.

Everybody seems to be at Washington, and yet there is a singular dearth of imperatively noticeable people there. I question whether there are half a dozen individuals, in all kinds of eminence, at whom a stranger, wearied with the contact of a hundred moderate celebrities, would turn round to snatch a second glance. Secretary Seward, to be sure, — a pale, large-nosed, elderly man, of moderate stature, with a decided originality of gait and aspect, and a cigar in his mouth, — etc., etc. [2]

[2] We are again compelled to interfere with our friend's license of personal description and criticism. Even Cabinet Ministers (to whom the next few pages of the article were devoted) had their private immunities, which ought to be conscientiously observed, — unless, indeed, the writer chanced to have some very piquant motives for violating them.

Of course, there was one other personage, in the class of statesmen, whom I should have been truly mortified to leave Washington without seeing; since (temporarily, at least, and by force of circumstances) he was the man of men. But a private grief had built up a barrier about him, impeding the customary free intercourse of Americans with their chief magistrate; so that I might have come away without a glimpse of his very remarkable physiognomy, save for a semi-official opportunity of which I was glad to take advantage. The fact is, we were invited to annex ourselves, as supernumeraries, to a deputation that was about to wait upon the President, from a Massachusetts whip-factory, with a present of a splendid whip.

Our immediate party consisted only of four or five (including Major Ben Perley Poore, with his notebook and pencil), but we were joined by several other persons, who seemed to have been lounging about the precincts of the White House, under the spacious porch, or within the hall, and who swarmed in with us to take the chances of a presentation. Nine o'clock had been appointed as the time for receiving the deputation, and we were punctual to the moment; but not so the President, who sent us word that he was eating his breakfast, and would come as soon as he could. His appetite, we were glad to think, must have been a pretty fair one; for we waited about half an hour in one of the antechambers, and then were ushered into a reception-room, in one corner of which sat the Secretaries of War and of the Treasury, expecting, like ourselves, the termination of the Presidential breakfast. During this interval there were several new additions to our group, one or two of whom were in a working-garb, so that we formed a very miscellaneous collection of people, mostly unknown to each other, and without any common sponsor, but all with an equal right to look our head-servant in the face.

By and by there was a little stir on the staircase and in the passage-way, and in lounged a tall, loose-jointed figure, of an exaggerated Yankee port and demeanor, whom (as being about the homeliest man I ever saw, yet by no means repulsive or disagreeable) it was impossible not to recognize as Uncle Abe. Unquestionably, Western man though he be, and Kentuckian by birth, President Lincoln is the essential representative of all Yankees, and the veritable specimen, physically, of what the world seems determined to regard as our characteristic qualities. It is the strangest and yet the fittest thing in the jumble of human vicissitudes, that he, out of so many millions, unlooked for, unselected by any intelligible process that could be based upon his genuine qualities, unknown to those who chose him, and unsuspected of what endowments may adapt him for his tremendous responsibility, should have found the way open for him to fling his lank personality into the chair of state, — where, I presume, it was his first impulse to throw his legs on the council-table, and tell the Cabinet Ministers a story. There is no describing his lengthy awkwardness, nor the uncouthness of his movement, and yet it seemed as if I had been in the habit of seeing him daily, and had shaken hands with him a thousand times in some village street; so true was he to the aspect of the pattern American, though with a certain extravagance which, possibly, I exaggerated still further by the delighted eagerness with which I took it in. If put to guess his calling and livelihood, I should have taken him for a country schoolmaster as soon as anything else. He was dressed in a rusty black frock-coat and pantaloons, unbrushed, and worn so faithfully that the suit had adapted itself to the curves and angularities of his figure, and had grown to be an outer skin of the man. He had shabby slippers on his feet. His hair was black, still unmixed with gray, stiff, somewhat bushy, and had apparently been acquainted with neither brush nor comb that morning, after the disarrangement of the pillow; and as to a night-cap, Uncle Abe probably knows nothing of such effeminacies. His complexion is dark and sallow, betokening, I fear, an insalubrious atmosphere around the White House; he has thick black eyebrows and an impending brow; his nose is large, and the lines about his mouth are very strongly defined. The whole physiognomy is as coarse a one as you would meet anywhere in the length and breadth of the States; but, withal, it is redeemed, illuminated, softened, and brightened by a kindly though serious look out of his eyes, and an expression of homely sagacity, that seems weighted with rich results of village experience. A great deal of native sense; no bookish cultivation, no refinement; honest at heart, and thoroughly so, and yet, in some sort, sly, — at least, endowed with a sort of tact and wisdom that are akin to craft, and would impel him, I think, to take an antagonist in flank rather than to make a bull-run at him right in front. But, on the whole, I like this sallow, queer, sagacious visage, with the homely human sympathies that warmed it; and, for my small share in the matter, would as lief have Uncle Abe for a ruler as any man whom it would have been practicable to put in his place.

Immediately on his entrance the President accosted our member of

Congress, who had us in charge, and, with a comical twist of his face, made some jocular remark about the length of his breakfast. He then greeted us all round, not waiting for an introduction, but shaking and squeezing everybody's hand with the utmost cordiality, whether the individual's name was announced to him or not. His manner towards us was wholly without pretence, but yet had a kind of natural dignity, quite sufficient to keep the forwardest of us from clapping him on the shoulder and asking him for a story. A mutual acquaintance being established, our leader took the whip out of its case, and began to read the address of presentation. The whip was an exceedingly long one, its handle wrought in ivory (by some artist in the Massachusetts State Prison, I believe), and ornamented with a medallion of the President, and other equally beautiful devices; and along its whole length there was a succession of golden bands and ferrules. The address was shorter than the whip, but equally well made, consisting chiefly of an explanatory description of these artistic designs, and closing with a hint that the gift was a suggestive and emblematic one, and that the President would recognize the use to which such an instrument should be put.

This suggestion gave Uncle Abe rather a delicate task in his reply, because, slight as the matter seemed, it apparently called for some declaration, or intimation, or faint foreshadowing of policy in reference to the conduct of the war, and the final treatment of the Rebels. But the President's Yankee aptness and not-to-be-caughtness stood him in good stead, and he jerked or wiggled himself out of the dilemma with an uncouth dexterity that was entirely in character; although, without his gesticulation of eye and mouth, — and especially the flourish of the whip, with which he imagined himself touching up a pair of fat horses, — I doubt whether his words would be worth recording, even if I could remember them. The gist of the reply was, that he accepted the whip as an emblem of peace, not punishment; and, this great affair over, we retired out of the presence in high good-humor, only regretting that we could not have seen the President sit down and fold up his legs (which is said to be a most extraordinary spectacle), or have heard him tell one of those delectable stories for which he is so celebrated. A good many of them are afloat upon the common talk of Washington, and are certainly the aptest, pithiest, and funniest little things imaginable; though, to be sure, they smack of the frontier freedom, and would not always bear repetition in a drawing-room, or on the immaculate page of the Atlantic. [3]

[3] [Note by G.P.L.:] The above passage relating to President Lincoln was one of those omitted from the article as originally published, and the following note was appended to explain the omission, which had been indicated by a line of points.

We are compelled to omit two or three pages in which the author describes the interview and gives his idea of the personal appearance and deportment of the President. The sketch appears to have been written in a benign spirit and perhaps conveys a not inaccurate impression of its august subject; but it lacks reverence, and it pains us to see a gentleman of ripe age, and who has spent years under the corrective influence of foreign institutions, falling into the characteristic and most ominous fault of Young America.

Good Heavens! What liberties have I been taking with one of the potentates of the earth, and the man on whose conduct more important consequences depend than on that of any other historical personage of the century! But with whom is an American citizen entitled to take a liberty, if not with his own chief magistrate? However, lest the above allusions to President Lincoln's little peculiarities (already well known to the country and to the world) should be misinterpreted, I deem it proper to say a word or two in regard to him, of unfeigned respect and measurable confidence. He is evidently a man of keen faculties, and, what is still more to the purpose, of powerful character. As to his integrity, the people have that intuition of it which is never deceived.

Before he actually entered upon his great office, and for a considerable time afterwards, there is no reason to suppose that he adequately estimated the gigantic task about to be imposed on him, or, at least, had any distinct idea how it was to be managed; and I presume there may have been more than one veteran politician who proposed to himself to take the power out of President Lincoln's hands into his own, leaving our honest friend only the public responsibility for the good or ill success of the career. The extremely imperfect development of his statesmanly qualities, at that period, may have justified such designs. But the President is teachable by events, and has now spent a year in a very arduous course of education; he has a flexible mind, capable of much expansion, and convertible towards far loftier studies and activities than those of his early life; and if he came to Washington a back-woods humorist, he has already transformed himself into as good a statesman (to speak moderately) as his prime-minister.

Among other excursions to camps and places of interest in the neighborhood of Washington, we went, one day, to Alexandria. It is a little port on the Potomac, with one or two shabby wharves and docks, resembling those of a fishing-village in New England, and the respectable old brick town rising gently behind. In peaceful times it no doubt bore an aspect of decorous quietude and dullness; but it was now thronged with the Northern soldiery, whose stir and bustle contrasted strikingly with the many closed warehouses, the absence of citizens from their customary haunts, and the lack of any symptom of healthy activity, while army-wagons trundled heavily over the pavements, and sentinels paced the sidewalks, and mounted dragoons dashed to and fro on military errands. I tried to imagine how very disagreeable the presence of a Southern army would be in a sober town of Massachusetts; and the thought considerably lessened my wonder at the cold and shy regards that are cast upon our troops, the gloom, the sullen demeanor, the declared or scarcely hidden sympathy with rebellion, which are so frequent here. It is a strange thing in human life, that the greatest errors both of men and women often spring from their sweetest and most generous qualities; and so, undoubtedly, thousands of warm-hearted, sympathetic, and impulsive persons have joined the Rebels, not from any real zeal for the cause, but because, between two conflicting loyalties, they chose that which necessarily lay nearest the heart. There never existed any other government against which treason was so easy, and could defend itself by such plausible arguments, as against that of the United States. The anomaly of two allegiances (of which that of the State comes nearest home to a man's feelings, and includes the altar and the hearth, while the General Government claims his devotion only to an airy mode of law, and has no symbol but a flag) is exceedingly mischievous in this point of view; for it has converted crowds of honest people into traitors, who seem to themselves not merely innocent, but patriotic, and who die for a bad cause with as quiet a conscience as if it were the best. In the vast extent of our country, — too vast by far to be taken into one small human heart, — we inevitably limit to our own State, or, at farthest, to our own section, that sentiment of physical love for the soil which renders an Englishman, for example, so intensely sensitive to the dignity and well-being of his little island, that one hostile foot, treading anywhere upon it, would make a bruise on each individual breast. If a man loves his own State, therefore, and is content to be ruined with her, let us shoot him, if we can, but allow him an honorable burial in the soil he fights for. [4]

[4] *We do not thoroughly comprehend the author's drift in the foregoing paragraph, but are inclined to think its tone reprehensible, and its tendency impolitic in the present stage of our national difficulties.*

In Alexandria, we visited the tavern in which Colonel Ellsworth was killed, and saw the spot where he fell, and the stairs below, whence Jackson fired the fatal shot, and where he himself was slain a moment afterwards; so that the assassin and his victim must have met on the threshold of the spirit-world, and perhaps came to a better understanding before they had taken many steps on the other side. Ellsworth was too generous to bear an immortal grudge for a deed like that, done in hot blood, and by no skulking enemy. The memorial-hunters have completely cut away the original wood-work around the spot, with their pocket-knives; and the staircase, balustrade, and floor, as well as the adjacent doors and door-frames, have recently been renewed; the walls, moreover, are covered with new paper-hangings, the former having been torn off in tatters; and thus it becomes something like a metaphysical question whether the place of the murder actually exists.

Driving out of Alexandria, we stopped on the edge of the city to inspect an old slave-pen, which is one of the lions of the place, but a very poor one; and a little farther on, we came to a brick church where Washington used sometimes to attend service, — a pre-Revolutionary edifice, with ivy growing over its walls, though not very luxuriantly. Reaching the open country, we saw forts and camps on all sides; some of the tents being placed immediately on the ground, while others were raised over a basement of logs, laid lengthwise, like those of a log-hut, or driven vertically into the soil in a circle, — thus forming a solid wall, the chinks

closed up with Virginia mud, and above it the pyramidal shelter of the tent. Here were in progress all the occupations, and all the idleness, of the soldier in the tented field; some were cooking the company-rations in pots hung over fires in the open air; some played at ball, or developed their muscular power by gymnastic exercise; some read newspapers; some smoked cigars or pipes; and many were cleaning their arms and accoutrements, — the more carefully, perhaps, because their division was to be reviewed by the Commander-in-Chief that afternoon; others sat on the ground, while their comrades cut their hair, — it being a soldierly fashion (and for excellent reasons) to crop it within an inch of the skull; others, finally, lay asleep in breast-high high tents, with their legs protruding into the open air.

We paid a visit to Fort Ellsworth, and from its ramparts (which have been heaped up out of the muddy soil within the last few months, and will require still a year or two to make them verdant) we had a beautiful view of the Potomac, a truly majestic river, and the surrounding country. The fortifications, so numerous in all this region, and now so unsightly with their bare, precipitous sides, will remain as historic monuments, grass-grown and picturesque memorials of an epoch of terror and suffering: they will serve to make our country dearer and more interesting to us, and afford fit soil for poetry to root itself in: for this is a plant which thrives best in spots where blood has been spilt long ago, and grows in abundant clusters in old ditches, such as the moat around Fort Ellsworth will be a century hence. It may seem to be paying dear for what many will reckon but a worthless weed; but the more historical associations we can link with our localities, the richer will be the daily life that feeds upon the past, and the more valuable the things that have been long established: so

that our children will be less prodigal than their fathers in sacrificing good institutions to passionate impulses and impracticable theories. This herb of grace, let us hope, may be found in the old footprints of the war.

Even in an aesthetic point of view, however, the war has done a great deal of enduring mischief, by causing the devastation of great tracts of woodland scenery, in which this part of Virginia would appear to have been very rich. Around all the encampments, and everywhere along the road, we saw the bare sites of what had evidently been tracts of hard-wood forest, indicated by the unsightly stumps of well-grown trees, not smoothly felled by regular axe-men, but hacked, haggled, and unevenly amputated, as by a sword, or other miserable tool, in an unskillful hand. Fifty years will not repair this desolation! An army destroys everything before and around it, even to the very grass; for the sites of the encamp-ments are converted into barren esplanades, like those of the squares in French cities, where not a blade of grass is allowed to grow. As to the other symptoms of devastation and obstruction, such as deserted houses, unfenced fields, and a general aspect of nakedness and ruin, I know not how much may be due to a normal lack of neatness in the rural life of Virginia, which puts a squalid face even upon a prosperous state of things; but undoubtedly the war must have spoilt what was good, and made the bad a great deal worse. The carcasses of horses were scattered along the wayside.

One very pregnant token of a social system thoroughly disturbed was presented by a party of contrabands, escaping out of the mysterious depths of Secessia; and its strangeness consisted in the leisurely delay with which they trudged forward, as dreading no pursuer, and encountering nobody to turn them back. They were unlike the specimens of their race whom we are accustomed to see at the North, and, in my judgment, were far more agreeable. So rudely were they attired, — as if their garb had grown upon them spontaneously, — so picturesquely natural in manners, and wearing such a crust of primeval simplicity (which is quite polished away from the northern black man), that they seemed a kind of creature by themselves, not altogether human, but perhaps quite as good, and akin to the fauns and rustic deities of olden times. I wonder whether I shall excite anybody's wrath by saying this. It is no great matter. At all events, I felt most kindly towards these poor fugitives, but knew not precisely what to wish in their behalf, nor in the least how to help them. For the sake of the manhood which is latent in them, I would not have turned them back; but I should have felt almost as reluctant, on their own account, to hasten them forward to the stranger's land; and I think my prevalent idea was, that, whoever may be benefited by the results of this war, it will not be the present generation of negroes, the childhood of whose race is now gone forever, and who must henceforth fight a hard battle with the world, on very unequal terms. On behalf of my own race, I am glad and can only hope that an inscrutable Providence means good to both parties.

There is an historical circumstance, known to few, that connects the children of the Puritans with these Africans of Virginia in a very singular way. They are our brethren, as being lineal descendants from the May-flower, the fated womb of which, in her first voyage, sent forth a brood of Pilgrims on Plymouth Rock, and, in a subsequent one, spawned slaves upon the Southern soil, — a monstrous birth, but with which we have an instinctive sense of kindred, and so are stirred by an irresistible impulse to attempt their rescue, even at the cost of blood and ruin. The character of our sacred ship, I fear, may suffer a little by this revelation; but we must let her white progeny offset her dark one, — and two such portents never sprang from an identical source before.

While we drove onward, a young officer on horseback looked earnestly into the carriage, and recognized some faces that he had seen before; so he rode along by our side, and we pestered him with queries and observations, to which he responded more civilly than they deserved. He was on General McClellan's staff, and a gallant cavalier, high-booted, with a revolver in his belt, and mounted on a noble horse, which trotted hard and high without disturbing the rider in his accustomed seat. His face had a healthy hue of exposure and an expression of careless hardihood; and, as I looked at him, it seemed to me that the war had brought good fortune to the youth of this epoch, if to none beside; since they now make it their daily business to ride a horse and handle a sword, instead of lounging listlessly through the duties, occupations, pleasures — all tedious alike — to which the artificial state of society limits a peaceful generation. The atmosphere of the camp and the smoke of the battlefield are morally invigorating; the hardy virtues flourish in them, the nonsense dies like a wilted weed. The enervating effects of centuries of civilization vanish at once, and leave these young men to enjoy a life of hardship, and the exhilarating sense of danger, — to kill men blame-

lessly, or to be killed gloriously, — and to be happy in following out their
native instincts of destruction, precisely in the spirit of Homer's heroes,
only with some considerable change of mode. One touch of Nature makes
not only the whole world, but all time, akin. Set men face to face, with
weapons in their hands, and they are as ready to slaughter one another
now, after playing at peace and good-will for so many years, as in the
rudest ages, that never heard of peace-societies, and thought no wine so
delicious as what they quaffed from an enemy's skull. Indeed, if the
report of a Congressional committee may be trusted, that old-fashioned
kind of goblet has again come into use, at the expense of our Northern
head-pieces, — a costly drinking-cup to him that furnishes it! Heaven
forgive me for seeming to jest upon such a subject! — only, it is so odd,
when we measure our advances from barbarism, and find ourselves
just here! [5]

[5] *We hardly expected this outbreak in favor of war from the Peaceable Man: but the justice of our
cause makes us all soldiers at heart, however quiet in our outward life. We have heard of twenty
Quakers in a single company of a Pennsylvania regiment.*

We now approached General McClellan's headquarters, which, at that
time, were established at Fairfield Seminary. The edifice was situated on
a gentle elevation, amid very agreeable scenery, and, at a distance, looked
like a gentleman's seat. Preparations were going forward for reviewing a
division of ten or twelve thousand men, the various regiments compos-
ing which had begun to array themselves on an extensive plain, where,
methought, there was a more convenient place for a battle than is usually
found in this broken and difficult country. Two thousand cavalry made a
portion of the troops to be reviewed. By and by we saw a pretty numerous troop of mounted officers, who were congregated on a distant part
of the plain, and whom we finally ascertained to be the Commander-in-
Chief's staff, with McClellan himself at their head. Our party managed
to establish itself in a position conveniently close to the General, to whom,
moreover, we had the honor of an introduction; and he bowed, on his
horseback, with a good deal of dignity and martial courtesy, but no airs
nor fuss nor pretension beyond what his character and rank inevitably
gave him.

Now, at that juncture, and, in fact, up to the present moment, there
was, and is, a most fierce and bitter outcry, and detraction loud and low,
against General McClellan, accusing him of sloth, imbecility, cowardice,

treasonable purposes, and, in short, utterly denying his ability as a soldier, and questioning his integrity as a man. Nor was this to be wondered at; for when before, in all history, do we find a general in command of half a million of men, and in presence of an enemy inferior in numbers and no better disciplined than his own troops, leaving it still debatable, after the better part of a year, whether he is a soldier or no? The question would seem to answer itself in the very asking. Nevertheless, being most profoundly ignorant of the art of war, like the majority of the General's critics, and, on the other hand, having some considerable impressibility by men's characters, I was glad of the opportunity to look him in the face, and to feel whatever influence might reach me from his sphere. So I stared at him, as the phrase goes, with all the eyes I had; and the reader shall have the benefit of what I saw, — to which he is the more welcome, because, in writing this article, I feel disposed to be singularly frank, and can scarcely restrain myself from telling truths the utterance of which I should get slender thanks for.

The General was dressed in a simple, dark-blue uniform, without epaulets, booted to the knee, and with a cloth cap upon his head; and, at first sight, you might have taken him for a corporal of dragoons, of particularly neat and soldier-like aspect, and in the prime of his age and strength. He is only of middling stature, but his build is very compact and sturdy, with broad shoulders and a look of great physical vigor, which, in fact, he is said to possess, — he and Beauregard having been rivals in that particular, and both distinguished above other men. His complexion is dark and sanguine, with dark hair. He has a strong, bold, soldierly face, full of decision; a Roman nose, by no means a thin prominence, but very thick and firm; and if he follows it (which I should think likely), it may be pretty confidently trusted to guide him aright. His profile would make a more effective likeness than the full face, which, however, is much better in the real man than in any photograph that I have seen. His forehead is not remarkably large, but comes forward at the eyebrows; it is not the brow nor countenance of a prominently intellectual man (not a natural student, I mean, or abstract thinker), but of one whose office it is to handle things practically and to bring about tangible results. His face looked capable of being very stern, but wore, in its repose, when I saw it, an aspect pleasant and dignified; it is not, in its character, an American face, nor an English one. The man on whom he fixes his eye is conscious of him. In his natural disposition, he seems calm and self-possessed, sustaining his great responsibilities cheerfully, without shrinking, or weariness, or spasmodic effort, or damage to his health, but all with quiet, deep-drawn breaths; just as his broad shoulders would bear up a heavy burden without aching beneath it.

After we had had sufficient time to peruse the man (so far as it could be done with one pair of very attentive eyes), the General rode off, followed by his cavalcade, and was lost to sight among the troops. They received him with loud shouts, by the eager uproar of which — now near, now in the centre, now on the outskirts of the division, and now sweeping back towards us in a great volume of sound — we could trace his progress through the ranks. If he is a coward, or a traitor, or a humbug, or anything less than a brave, true, and able man, that mass of intelligent soldiers, whose lives and honor he had in charge, were utterly deceived, and so was this present writer; for they believed in him, and so did I; and had I stood in the ranks, I should have shouted with the lustiest of them. Of course I may be mistaken; my opinion on such a point is worth nothing, although my impression may be worth a little more; neither do I consider the General's antecedents as bearing very decided testimony to his practical soldiership. A thorough knowledge of the science of war seems to be conceded to him; he is allowed to be a good military critic; but all this is possible without his possessing any positive qualities of a great general, just as a literary critic may show the profoundest acquaintance with the principles of epic poetry without being able to produce a single stanza of an epic poem. Nevertheless, I shall not give up my faith in General McClellan's soldiership until he is defeated, nor in his courage and integrity even then.

Another of our excursions was to Harper's Ferry, — the Directors of the Baltimore and Ohio Railroad having kindly invited us to accompany them on the first trip over the newly laid track, after its breaking up by the Rebels. It began to rain, in the early morning, pretty soon after we left Washington, and continued to pour a cataract throughout the day; so that the aspect of the country was dreary, where it would otherwise have been delightful, as we entered among the hill-scenery that is formed by the subsiding swells of the Alleghanies. The latter part of our journey lay along the shore of the Potomac, in its upper course, where the margin of that noble river is bordered by gray, overhanging crags, beneath which

— and sometimes right through them — the railroad takes its way. In one place the Rebels had attempted to arrest a train by precipitating an immense mass of rock down upon the track, by the side of which it still lay, deeply imbedded in the ground, and looking as if it might have lain there since the Deluge. The scenery grew even more picturesque as we proceeded, the bluffs becoming very bold in their descent upon the river, which, at Harper's Ferry, presents as striking a vista among the hills as a painter could desire to see. But a beautiful landscape is a luxury, and luxuries are thrown away amid discomfort; and when we alighted into the tenacious mud and almost fathomless puddle, on the hither side of the Ferry (the ultimate point to which the cars proceeded, since the railroad bridge had been destroyed by the Rebels), I cannot remember that any very rapturous emotions were awakened by the scenery.

We paddled and floundered over the ruins of the track, and, scrambling down an embankment, crossed the Potomac by a pontoon-bridge, a thousand feet in length, over the narrow line of which — level with the river, and rising and subsiding with it — General Banks had recently led his whole army, with its ponderous artillery and heavily laden wagons. Yet our own tread made it vibrate. The broken bridge of the railroad was a little below us, and at the base of one of its massive piers, in the rocky bed of the river, lay a locomotive, which the Rebels had precipitated there. As we passed over, we looked towards the Virginia shore, and beheld the little town of Harper's Ferry, gathered about the base of a round hill and climbing up its steep acclivity; so that it somewhat resembled the Etruscan cities which I have seen among the Apennines, rushing, as it were, down an apparently breakneck height. About midway of the ascent stood a shabby brick church, towards which a difficult path went scrambling up the precipice, indicating, one would say, a very fervent aspiration on the part of the worshippers, unless there was some easier mode of access in another direction. Immediately on the shore of the Potomac, and extending back towards the town, lay the dismal ruins of the United States arsenal and armory, consisting of piles of broken bricks and a waste of shapeless demolition, amid which we saw gun-barrels in heaps of hundreds together. They were the relics of the conflagration, bent with the heat of the fire and rusted with the wintry rain to which they had since been exposed. The brightest sunshine could not have made the scene cheerful, nor have taken away the gloom from the dilapidated town; for, besides the natural shabbiness, and decayed, unthrifty look of a Virginian village, it has an inexpressible forlornness resulting from the devastations of war and its occupation by both armies alternately. Yet there would be a less striking contrast between Southern and New England villages, if the former were as much in the habit of using white paint as we are. It is prodigiously efficacious in putting a bright face upon a bad matter.

There was one small shop, which appeared to have nothing for sale. A single man and one or two boys were all the inhabitants in view, except the Yankee sentinels and soldiers, belonging to Massachusetts regiments, who were scattered about pretty numerously. A guard-house stood on the slope of the hill; and in the level street at its base were the offices of the Provost-Marshal and other military authorities, to whom we forthwith reported ourselves. The Provost-Marshal kindly sent a corporal to guide us to the little building which John Brown seized upon as his fortress, and which, after it was stormed by the United States marines, became his temporary prison. It is an old engine-house, rusty and shabby, like every other work of man's hands in this God-forsaken town, and stands fronting upon the river, only a short distance from the bank, nearly at the point where the pontoon-bridge touches the Virginia shore. In its front wall, on each side of the door, are two or three ragged loop-holes, which John Brown perforated for his defence, knocking out merely a brick or two, so as to give himself and his garrison a sight over their rifles. Through these orifices the sturdy old man dealt a good deal of deadly mischief among his assailants, until they broke down the door by thrusting against it with a ladder, and tumbled headlong in upon him. I shall not pretend to be an admirer of old John Brown, any farther than sympathy with Whittier's excellent ballad about him may go; nor did I expect ever to shrink so unutterably from any apophthegm of a sage, whose happy lips have uttered a hundred golden sentences, as from that saying (perhaps falsely attributed to so honored a source), that the death of this blood-stained fanatic has "made the Gallows as venerable as the Cross!" Nobody was ever more justly hanged. He won his martyrdom fairly, and took it firmly. He himself, I am persuaded (such was his natural integrity), would have acknowledged that Virginia had a right to take the life which he had staked and lost; although it would have been better for her, in the hour that is fast coming, if she could generously have forgotten the criminality of his attempt in its enormous folly. On the other hand, any common-sensible man, looking at the matter unsentimentally, must have felt a certain intellectual satisfaction in seeing him hanged, if it were only in requital of his preposterous miscalculation of possibilities. [6]

[6] *Can it be a son of old Massachusetts who utters this abominable sentiment? For shame.*

But, coolly as I seem to say these things, my Yankee heart stirred triumphantly when I saw the use to which John Brown's fortress and prison-house has now been put. What right have I to complain of any other man's foolish impulses, when I cannot possibly control my own? The engine-house is now a place of confinement for Rebel prisoners.

A Massachusetts soldier stood on guard, but readily permitted our whole party to enter. It was a wretched place. A room of perhaps twenty-five feet square occupied the whole interior of the building, having an iron stove in its centre, whence a rusty funnel ascended towards a hole in the roof, which served the purposes of ventilation, as well as for the exit of smoke. We found ourselves right in the midst of the Rebels, some of whom lay on heaps of straw, asleep, or, at all events, giving no sign of consciousness; others sat in the corners of the room, huddled close together, and staring with a lazy kind of interest at the visitors; two were astride of some planks, playing with the dirtiest pack of cards that I ever happened to see. There was only one figure in the least military among all these twenty prisoners of war, — a man with a dark, intelligent moustached face, wearing a shabby cotton uniform, which he had contrived to arrange with a degree of soldierly smartness, though it had evidently borne the brunt of a very filthy campaign. He stood erect, and talked freely with those who addressed him, telling them his place of residence, the number of his regiment, the circumstances of his capture, and such other

particulars as their Northern inquisitiveness prompted them to ask. I
liked the manliness of his deportment; he was neither ashamed, nor afraid,
nor in the slightest degree sullen, peppery, or contumacious, but bore
himself as if whatever animosity he had felt towards his enemies was left
upon the battle-field, and would not be resumed till he had again a weapon
in his hand.

Neither could I detect a trace of hostile feeling in the countenance,
words, or manner of any prisoner there. Almost to a man, they were
simple, bumpkin-like fellows, dressed in homespun clothes, with faces
singularly vacant of meaning, but sufficiently good-humored a breed of
men, in short, such as I did not suppose to exist in this country, although
I have seen their like in some other parts of the world. They were peasants,
and of a very low order: a class of people with whom our Northern rural
population has not a single trait in common. They were exceedingly respectful, — more so than a rustic New-Englander ever dreams of being towards
anybody, except perhaps his minister; and had they worn any hats, they
would probably have been self-constrained to take them off, under the
unusual circumstance of being permitted to hold conversation with well-
dressed persons. It is my belief that not a single bumpkin of them all (the
moustached soldier always excepted) had the remotest comprehension
of what they had been fighting for, or how they had deserved to be shut
up in that dreary hole; nor, possibly, did they care to inquire into this
latter mystery, but took it as a godsend to be suffered to lie here in a heap
of unwashed human bodies, well warmed and well foddered to-day, and
without the necessity of bothering themselves about the possible hunger
and cold of tomorrow. Their dark prison-life may have seemed to them
the sunshine of all their lifetime.

There was one poor wretch, a wild-beast of a man, at whom I gazed
with greater interest than at his fellows; although I know not that each
one of them, in their semi-barbarous moral state, might not have been
capable of the same savage impulse that had made this particular individual a horror to all beholders. At the close of some battle or skirmish, a
wounded Union soldier had crept on hands and knees to his feet, and
besought his assistance, — not dreaming that any creature in human
shape, in the Christian land where they had so recently been brethren,
could refuse it. But this man (this fit fiend, if you prefer to call him so,
though I would not advise it) flung a bitter curse at the poor Northerner,

and absolutely trampled the soul out of his body, as he lay writhing beneath his feet. The fellow's face was horribly ugly; but I am not quite sure that I should have noticed it, if I had not known his story. He spoke not a word, and met nobody's eye, but kept staring upward into the smoky vacancy towards the ceiling, where, it might be, he beheld a continual portraiture of his victim's horror-stricken agonies. I rather fancy, however, that his moral sense was yet too torpid to trouble him with such remorseful visions, and that, for his own part, he might have had very agreeable reminiscences of the soldier's death, if other eyes had not been bent reproachfully upon him and warned him that something was amiss. It was this reproach in other men's eyes that made him look aside. He was a wild-beast, as I began with saying, — an unsophisticated wild-beast, — while the rest of us are partially tamed, though still the scent of blood excites some of the savage instincts of our nature. What this wretch needed, in order to make him capable of the degree of mercy and benevolence that exists in us, was simply such a measure of moral and intellectual development as we have received; and, in my mind, the present war is so well justified by no other consideration as by the probability that it will free this class of Southern whites from a thralldom in which they scarcely begin to be responsible beings. So far as the education of the heart is concerned, the negroes have apparently the advantage of them; and as to other schooling, it is practically unattainable by black or white.

Looking round at these poor prisoners, therefore, it struck me as an immense absurdity that they should fancy us their enemies; since, whether we intend it so or no, they have a far greater stake on our success than we can possibly have. For ourselves, the balance of advantages between defeat and triumph may admit of question. For them, all truly valuable things are dependent on our complete success; for thence would come the regeneration of a people, — the removal of a foul scurf that has overgrown their life, and keeps them in a state of disease and decrepitude, one of the chief symptoms of which is, that, the more they suffer and are debased, the more they imagine themselves strong and beautiful. No human effort, on a grand scale, has ever yet resulted according to the purpose of its projectors. The advantages are always incidental. Man's accidents are God's purposes. We miss the good we sought, and do the good we little cared for. [7]

[7] *The author seems to imagine that he has compressed a great deal of meaning into these little,*

hard, dry pellets of aphoristic wisdom. We disagree with him. The counsels of wise and good men
are often coincident with the purposes of Providence; and the present war promises to illustrate
our remark.

Our Government evidently knows when and where to lay its finger upon its most available citizens; for, quite unexpectedly, we were joined with some other gentlemen, scarcely less competent than ourselves, in a commission to proceed to Fortress Monroe and examine into things in general. Of course, official propriety compels us to be extremely guarded in our description of the interesting objects which this expedition opened to our view. There can be no harm, however, in stating that we were received by the commander of the fortress with a kind of acid good-nature, or mild cynicism, that indicated him to be a humorist, character-ized by certain rather pungent peculiarities, yet of no unamiable cast. He is a small, thin old gentleman, set off by a large pair of brilliant epaulets, — the only pair, so far as my observation went, that adorn the shoulders of any officer in the Union army. Either for our inspection, or because the matter had already been arranged, he drew out a regiment of Zouaves that formed the principal part of his garrison, and appeared at their head, sitting on horseback with rigid perpendicularity, and affording us a vivid idea of the disciplinarian of Baron Steuben's school.

There can be no question of the General's military qualities; he must have been especially useful in converting raw recruits into trained and efficient soldiers. But valor and martial skill are of so evanescent a character (hardly less fleeting than a woman's beauty), that Government has perhaps taken the safer course in assigning to this gallant officer, though distinguished in former wars, no more active duty than the guard-ianship of an apparently impregnable fortress. The ideas of military men solidify and fossilize so fast, while military science makes such rapid advances, that even here there might be a difficulty. An active, diversi-fied, and therefore a youthful, ingenuity is required by the quick exigencies of this singular war. Fortress Monroe, for example, in spite of the massive solidity of its ramparts, its broad and deep moat, and all the contrivances of defence that were known at the not very remote epoch of its construction, is now pronounced absolutely incapable of resisting the novel modes of assault which may be brought to bear upon it. It can only be the flexible talent of a young man that will evolve a new efficiency out of its obsolete strength.

It is a pity that old men grow unfit for war, not only by their incapacity for new ideas, but by the peaceful and unadventurous tendencies that gradually possess themselves of the once turbulent disposition, which used to snuff the battle-smoke as its congenial atmosphere. It is a pity, because it would be such an economy of human existence, if time-stricken people (whose value I have the better right to estimate, as reckoning myself one of them) could snatch from their juniors the exclusive privilege of carrying on the war. In case of death upon the battle-field, how unequal would be the comparative sacrifice! On one part, a few unenjoyable years, the little remnant of a life grown torpid; on the many fervent summers of manhood in its spring and prime, with all that they include of possible benefit to mankind. Then, too, a bullet offers such a brief and easy way, such a pretty little orifice, through which the weary spirit might seize the opportunity to be exhaled! If I had the ordering of these matters, fifty should be the tenderest age at which a recruit might be accepted for training; at fifty-five or sixty, I would consider him eligible for most kinds of military duty and exposure, excluding, that of a forlorn hope, which no soldier should be permitted to volunteer upon, short of the ripe age of seventy. As a general rule, these venerable combatants should have the preference for all dangerous and honorable service in the order of their seniority, with a distinction in favor of those whose infirmities might render their lives less worth the keeping. Methinks there would be no more Bull Runs; a warrior with gout in his toe, or rheumatism in his joints, or with one foot in the grave, would make a sorry fugitive!

On this admirable system, the productive part of the population would be undisturbed even by the bloodiest war; and, best of all, those thousands upon thousands of our Northern girls, whose proper mates will perish in camp-hospitals or on Southern battle-fields, would avoid their doom of forlorn old-maidenhood. But, no doubt, the plan will be pooh-poohed down by the War Department; though it could scarcely be more disastrous than the one on which we began the war, when a young army was struck with paralysis through the age of its commander.

The waters around Fortress Monroe were thronged with a gallant array of ships of war and transports, wearing the Union flag, — "Old Glory," as I hear it called in these days. A little withdrawn from our national fleet lay two French frigates, and, in another direction, an English sloop, under that banner which always makes itself visible, like a red portent in the air, wherever there is strife. In pursuance of our official duty (which had no ascertainable limits), we went on board the flag-ship, and were shown over every part of her, and down into her depths, inspecting her gallant crew, her powerful armament, her mighty engines, and her furnaces, where the fires are always kept burning, as well at midnight as at noon, so that it would require only five minutes to put the vessel under full steam. This vigilance has been felt necessary ever since the Merrimack made that terrible dash from Norfolk. Splendid as she is, however, and provided with all but the very latest improvements in naval armament, the Minnesota belongs to a class of vessels that will be built no more, nor ever fight another battle, — being as much a thing, of the past as any of the ships of Queen Elizabeth's time, which grappled with the galleons of the Spanish Armada.

On her quarter-deck, an elderly flag-officer was pacing to and fro, with a self-conscious dignity to which a touch of the gout or rheumatism perhaps contributed a little additional stiffness. He seemed to be a gallant gentleman, but of the old, slow, and pompous school of naval worthies, who have grown up amid rules, forms and etiquette which were adopted full-blown from the British navy into ours, and are somewhat too cumbrous for the quick spirit of today. This order of nautical heroes will probably go down, along with the ships in which they fought valorously and strutted most intolerably. How can an admiral condescend to go to sea in an iron pot? What space and elbow-room can be found for quarter-deck dignity in the cramped lookout of the Monitor, or even in the twenty-feet diameter of her cheese-box? All the pomp and splendor of naval warfare are gone by. Henceforth there must come up a race of enginemen and smoke-blackened cannoneers, who will hammer away at their enemies under the direction of a single pair of eyes; and even heroism — so deadly a gripe is Science laying on our noble possibilities — will become a quality of very minor importance, when its possessor cannot break through the iron crust of his own armament and give the world a glimpse of it.

At no great distance from the Minnesota lay the strangest-looking craft I ever saw. It was a platform of iron, so nearly on a level with the water that the swash of the waves broke over it, under the impulse of a very moderate breeze; and on this platform was raised a circular structure, likewise of iron, and rather broad and capacious, but of no great height. It could not be called a vessel at all; it was a machine, — and I have seen one of somewhat similar appearance employed in cleaning out the docks, or, for lack of a better similitude, it looked like a gigantic rat-trap. It was ugly, questionable, suspicious, evidently mischievous, — nay, I will allow myself to call it devilish; for this was the new war-fiend, destined, along with others of the same breed, to annihilate whole navies and batter down old supremacies. The wooden walls of Old England cease to exist, and a whole history of naval renown reaches its period, now that the Monitor comes smoking into view; while the billows dash over what seems her deck, and storms bury even her turret in green water, as she burrows and snorts along, oftener under the surface than above. The singularity of the object has betrayed me into a more ambitious vein of description than I often indulge; and, after all, I might as well have contented myself with simply saying that she looked very queer.

Going on board, we were surprised at the extent and convenience of her interior accommodations. There is a spacious ward-room, nine or ten feet in height, besides a private cabin for the commander, and sleeping accommodations on an ample scale; the whole well lighted and ventilated, though beneath the surface of the water. Forward, or aft (for it is impossible to tell stem from stern), the crew are relatively quite as well provided for as the officers. It was like finding a palace, with all its conveniences, under the sea. The inaccessibility, the apparent impregnability, of this submerged iron fortress are most satisfactory; the officers and crew get down through a little hole in the deck, hermetically seal themselves, and go below; and until they see fit to reappear, there would seem to be no power given to man whereby they can be brought to light. A storm of cannon-shot damages them no more than a handful of dried peas. We saw the shot-marks made by the great artillery of the Merrimack on the outer casing of the iron tower; they were about the breadth and depth of shallow saucers, almost imperceptible dents, with no corresponding bulge on the interior surface. In fact, the thing looked altogether too safe; though it may not prove quite an agreeable predicament to be thus boxed up in impenetrable iron, with the possibility, one would imagine, of being sent to the bottom of the sea, and, even there, not drowned, but stifled. Nothing, however, can exceed the confidence of the officers in this new craft. It was pleasant to see their benign exultation in her powers of mischief, and the delight with which they exhibited the circumvolutory movement of the tower, the quick thrusting forth of the immense guns to deliver their ponderous missiles, and then the immediate recoil, and the security behind the closed port-holes. Yet even this will not long be the last and most terrible improvement in the science of war. Already we hear of vessels the armament which is to act entirely beneath the surface of the water; so that, with no other external symptoms than a great bubbling and foaming, and gush of smoke, and belch of smothered thunder out of the yeasty waves, there shall be a deadly fight going on below, — and, by and by, a sucking whirlpool, as one of the ships goes down.

The Monitor was certainly an object of great interest; but on our way to Newport News, whither we next went, we saw a spectacle that affected us with far profounder emotion. It was the sight of the few sticks that are left of the frigate Congress, stranded near the shore, — and still more, the masts of the Cumberland rising midway out of the water, with a tattered rag of a pennant fluttering from one of them. The invisible hull of the latter ship seems to be careened over, so that the three masts stand slantwise; the rigging looks quite unimpaired, except that a few ropes dangle loosely from the yards. The flag (which never was struck, thank Heaven!) is entirely hidden under the waters of the bay, but is still doubtless waving in its old place, although it floats to and fro with the swell and reflux of the tide, instead of rustling on the breeze. A remnant of the dead crew still man the sunken ship, and sometimes a drowned body floats up to the surface.

That was a noble fight. When was ever a better word spoken than that of Commodore Smith, the father of the commander of the Congress, when he heard that his son's ship was surrendered? "Then Joe's dead!" said he; and so it proved. Nor can any warrior be more certain of enduring renown than the gallant Morris, who fought so well the final battle of the old system of naval warfare, and won glory for his country and himself out of inevitable disaster and defeat. That last gun from the Cumberland, when her deck was half submerged, sounded the requiem of many sinking ships. Then went down all the navies of Europe, and our own, Old Ironsides and all, and Trafalgar and a thousand other fights became only a memory, never to be acted over again; and thus our brave countrymen come last in the long procession of heroic sailors that includes Blake and Nelson, and so many mariners of England, and other mariners as brave as they, whose renown is our native inheritance. There will be other battles, but no more such tests of seamanship and manhood as the battles of the past; and, moreover, the Millennium is certainly approaching, because human strife is to be transferred from the heart and personality of man into cunning contrivances of machinery, which by and by will fight out our wars with only the clank and smash of iron, strewing the field with broken engines, but damaging nobody's little finger except by accident. Such is obviously the tendency of modern improvement. But, in the meanwhile, so long as manhood retains any part of its pristine value, no country can afford to let gallantry like that of Morris and his crew, any more than that of the brave Worden, pass unhonored and unrewarded. If the Government do nothing, let the people take the matter into their own hands, and cities give him swords, gold boxes, festivals of triumph, and, if he needs it, heaps of gold. Let poets brood upon the theme, and make themselves sensible how much of the past and future is contained within its compass, till its spirit shall flash forth in the lightning of a song!

From these various excursions, and a good many others (including one to Manassas), we gained a pretty lively idea of what was going on; but, after all, if compelled to pass a rainy day in the hall and parlors of Willard's Hotel, it proved about as profitably spent as if we had floundered miles of Virginia mud, in quest of interesting matter. This hotel, in fact, may be much more justly called the centre of Washington and the Union than either the Capitol, the White House, or the State Department. Everybody may be seen there. It is the meeting-place of the true representatives of the country, — not such as are chosen blindly and amiss by electors who take a folded ballot from the hand of a local politician, and thrust it into the ballot-box unread, but men who gravitate or are attracted hither by real business, or a native impulse to breathe the intensest atmosphere of the nation's life, or a genuine anxiety to see how this life-and-death struggle is going to deal with us. Nor these only, but all manner of loafers. Never, in any other spot, was there such a miscellany of people. You exchange nods with governors of sovereign States; you elbow illustrious men, and tread on the toes of generals; you hear statesmen and orators speaking in their familiar tones. You are mixed up with office-seekers, wire-pullers, inventors, artists, poets, prosers (including editors, army-correspondents, attachés of foreign journals, and long-winded talkers), clerks, diplomatists, mail-contractors, railway-directors, until your own identity is lost among them. Occasionally you talk with a man whom you have never before heard of, and are struck by the brightness of a thought, and fancy that there is more wisdom hidden among the obscure than is anywhere revealed among the famous. You adopt the universal habit of the place, and call for a mint-julep, a whiskey-skin, a gin-cocktail, a brandy-smash, or a glass of pure Old Rye; for the conviviality of Washington sets in at an early hour, and, so far as I had an opportunity of observing, never terminates at any hour, and all these drinks are continually in request by almost all these people. A constant atmosphere of cigar-smoke, too, envelops the motley crowd, and forms a sympathetic medium, in which men meet more closely and talk more frankly than in any other kind of air. If legislators would smoke in session, they might speak truer words, and fewer of them, and bring about more valuable results.

It is curious to observe what antiquated figures and costumes some-times make their appearance at Willard's. You meet elderly men with frilled shirt-fronts, for example, the fashion of which adornment passed away from among the people of this world half a century ago. It is as if one of Stuart's portraits were walking abroad. I see no way of accounting for this, except that the trouble of the times, the impiety of traitors, and the peril of our sacred Union and Constitution have disturbed, in their hon-ored graves, some of the venerable fathers of the country, and summoned them forth to protest against the meditated and half-accomplished sacrilege. If it be so, their wonted fires are not altogether extinguished in their ashes, — in their throats, I might rather say, — for I beheld one of these excellent old men quaffing such a horn of Bourbon whiskey as a toper the present century would be loath to venture upon. But, really, one would be glad to know where these strange figures come from. It shows, at any rate, how many remote, decaying villages and country-neighborhoods of the North, and forest-nooks of the West, and old mansion-houses in cities, are shaken by the tremor of our native soil, so that men long hidden in retirement put on the garments of their youth and hurry out to inquire what is the matter. The old men whom we see here have generally more marked faces than the young ones, and natu-rally enough; since it must be an extraordinary vigor and renewability of life that can overcome the rusty sloth of age, and keep the senior flexible enough to take an interest in new things; whereas hundreds of commonplace young men come hither to stare with eyes of vacant wonder, and with vague hopes of finding out what they are fit for. And this war (we may say so much in its favor) has been the means of discovering that important secret to not a few.

We saw at Willard's many who had thus found out for themselves, that, when Nature gives a young man no other utilizable faculty, she must be understood as intending him for a soldier. The bulk of the army had moved out of Washington before we reached the city; yet it seemed to me that at least two thirds of the guests and idlers at the hotel wore one or another token of the military profession. Many of them, no doubt, were self-commissioned officers, and had put on the buttons and the shoulder-straps, and booted themselves to the knees, merely because captain, in these days, is so good a traveling-name. The majority, however, had been duly appointed by the president, but might be none the better warriors for that. It was pleasant, occasionally, to distinguish veteran among this crowd of carpet-knights, — the trained soldier of a lifetime, long ago from West Point, who had spent his prime upon the frontier, and very likely could show an Indian bullet-mark on his breast, — if such decorations, won in an obscure warfare, were worth the showing now.

The question often occurred to me, — and, to say the truth, it added an indefinable piquancy to the scene, — what proportion of all these people, whether soldiers or civilians, were true at heart to the Union, and what part were tainted, more or less, with treasonable sympathies and wishes, even if such had never blossomed into purpose. Traitors there were among them, — no doubt of that, — civil servants of the public. Very reputable persons, who yet deserved to dangle from a cord; or men who buttoned military coats over their breasts, hiding perilous secrets there, which might bring the gallant officer to stand pale-faced before a file of musketeers, with his open grave behind him. But, without insisting upon such picturesque criminality and punishment as this, an observer, who kept both his eyes and heart open, would find it by no means difficult to discern that many residents and visitors of Washington so far sided with the South as to desire nothing more nor better than to see everything re-established a little worse than its former basis. If the cabinet of Richmond were transferred to the Federal city, and the North awfully snubbed, at least, and driven back within its old political limits, they would deem it a happy day. It is no wonder, and, if we look at the matter generously, no unpardonable crime.

Very excellent people hereabouts remember the many dynasties in which the Southern character has been predominant, and contrast the genial courtesy, the warm and graceful freedom of that region, with what they call (though I utterly disagree with them) the frigidity of our Northern manners, and the Western plainness of the President. They have a conscientious, though mistaken belief that the South was driven out of the Union by intolerable wrong on our part, and that we are responsible for having compelled true patriots to love only half their country instead of the whole, and brave soldiers to draw their swords against the Constitution which they would once have died for, — to draw them, too, with a bitterness of animosity which is the only symptom of brotherhood (since brothers hate each other best) that any longer exists. They whisper these things with tears in their eyes, and shake their heads, and stoop their poor old shoulders, at the tidings of another and another Northern victory, which, in their opinion, puts farther off the remote, the already impossible, chance of a reunion.

I am sorry for them, though it is by no means a sorrow without hope. Since the matter has gone so far, there seems to be no way but to go on winning victories, and establishing peace and a truer union in another generation, at the expense, probably, of greater trouble, in the present one, than any other people ever voluntarily suffered. We woo the South "as the Lion woos his bride;" it is a rough courtship, but perhaps love and a quiet household may come of it at last. Or, if we stop short of that blessed consummation, heaven was heaven still, as Milton sings, after Lucifer and a third part of the angels had seceded from its golden palaces, — and perhaps all the more heavenly, because so many gloomy brows, and soured, vindictive hearts, had gone to plot ineffectual schemes of mischief elsewhere. [8]

[8] We regret the innuendo in the concluding sentence. The war can never be allowed to terminate, except in the complete triumph of Northern principles. We hold the event in our own hands, and may choose whether to terminate it by the methods already so successfully used, or by other means equally within our control, and calculated to be still more speedily efficacious. In truth, the work is already done.

We should be sorry to cast a doubt on the Peaceable Man's loyalty, but he will allow us to say that we consider him premature in his kindly feelings towards traitors and sympathizers with treason.

As the author himself says of John Brown (and, so applied, we thought it an atrociously cold-blooded dictum), "any common-sensible man would feel an intellectual satisfaction in seeing them hanged, were it only for their preposterous miscalculation of possibilities."

There are some degrees of absurdity that put Reason herself into a rage, and affect us like an intolerable crime, — which this Rebellion is, into the bargain.

Hawthorne as War Correspondent

By Tom Wicker

Most literary artists have seen presidents only at a distance, or under awestricken circumstances, or on such formal occasions as when John F. Kennedy invited all living Nobel Prize winners to the White House — an evening, JFK remarked, that brought to the president's mansion the largest collection of talents to gather there "since Thomas Jefferson dined alone." But in 1862 one of the nation's most renowned writers, Nathaniel Hawthorne, had a rare up-close-and-almost-personal encounter with perhaps the greatest American president, Abraham Lincoln.

Naturally, editors being what they are, James T. Fields of the *Atlantic Monthly* chose to cut Hawthorne's comments on Lincoln from "Chiefly About War Matters,"[1] one of the novelist's few excursions into journalism. Fields evidently bowed to his nineteenth-century idea of political correctness, writing Hawthorne: "It will be politic to alter yr. phrases with reference to the President to leave out the description of his awkwardness & general uncouth aspect . . . the monkey figure of 'Uncle Abe' as he appears in yr. paper."

Hawthorne wondered "with whom is an American citizen entitled to take a liberty, if not with his own chief magistrate?" The author of *The Scarlet Letter* also wrote Fields: "I really think you omit the only part of the article worth publishing. Upon my honor, it seemed to me to have a historical value." But then, sounding like many a lesser writer in all ages, including our own, he added mildly: "Let it go."

Historical value, indeed! To my knowledge, no other great president has been so perceptively scrutinized by so great a writer (of course, all presidents today are so often seen on television that their exterior is more familiar to us than that of, say, the mayor or the local member of Congress). Hawthorne's article later was published in full but in July 1862, *Atlantic* readers were denied the novelist's shrewd appraisal of their much maligned president (as he was then):

"A great deal of native sense; no bookish cultivation, no refinement; honest at heart, and thoroughly so, and yet, in some sort, sly, — at least, endowed with a sort of tact and wisdom that are akin to craft, and would impel him, I think, to take an antagonist in flank than to make a bull-run at him right in front."

Such splendid figures of the time as Secretary of State Seward, General-in-Chief McClellan and Secretary of the Treasury Salmon P. Chase, among others, learned from hard experience the truth of Hawthorne's instinctive judgment of "Uncle Abe's" political skills.

The writer took no active part in the Civil War but remained throughout it mostly at Wayside, his home in Concord, Massachusetts. Believing at one point, however, that "there is a kind of treason in insulating one's self from the universal fear and sorrow," he set off in 1862 for his single trip to the theater of war, which became the basis for his essay, "Chiefly About War Matters." On his trip south, he was accompanied by a friend, William Ticknor (Fields's partner at the *Atlantic* and in publishing, which suggests that Hawthorne may have been "assigned" to war coverage by the magazine).

Among other leading figures he encountered and pictured with a writer's attention to detail was Secretary Seward ("a pale, large-nosed, elderly man, of moderate stature, with a decided originality of gait and aspect, and a cigar in his mouth") and the Union commander in chief, McClellan, who was about to begin his ill-fated Peninsula Campaign. In the general's case, Hawthorne — like many a journalist before and after him — relied too heavily on appearance. Observing "the Little Napoleon" reviewing a division, he was overly impressed: "If [McClellan] is a coward, or a traitor, or a humbug, or anything less than a brave, true and able man, [his cheering troops] were utterly deceived, and so was this present writer; for they believed in him, and so did I; and had I stood in the ranks, I should have shouted with the lustiest of them ... I shall not give up my faith in General McClellan's soldiership until he is defeated, nor in his courage and integrity even then." That moment was less than a year in coming; by the end of 1862, after the bloody battle at Antietam, civilians like Hawthorne had reason to agree with President Lincoln that McClellan had a bad case of "the slows" and should be dismissed.

Despite his fame, Hawthorne did not prove to be a "big foot" journalist, as colleagues call them today — one who interviews high officials, reads the communiqués, lives well and stays away from the front. He visited the camps, seeing "all the occupations, and all the idleness, of soldiers in the tented fields;" and observed that "an Army destroys everything before and around it," citing "the bare sites of what had evidently been tracts of hardwood forest ... the unsightly stumps of well-grown trees, not smoothly felled by regular axe-men, but hacked, haggled and unevenly amputated as by a sword ... in an unskilled hand. Fifty years will not repair this desolation!" Laconically, he noted also "the carcasses of horses ... scattered along the wayside."

Venturing by rail to Harper's Ferry, which in those days was on the very frontier of "Secessia," Hawthorne rode over newly laid rails replacing those torn up by Confederates, and arrived at a Potomac river bridge they had just destroyed. He crossed the river in a wintry rainfall, on a pontoon structure "arising and subsiding" with the flow of the current, and saw that "the brightest sunshine could not have made the scene cheerful, nor have taken away the gloom from the dilapidated town," or the "inexpressible forlornness resulting from the devastations of war and its occupation by both armies alternately."

The old Harper's Ferry engine-house, where John Brown had made his doomed stand, evoked from Hawthorne — a moderate in politics — the harsh judgment that "nobody was ever more justly hanged" than "this blood-stained fanatic." He rejected, too, an overblown tribute by his colleague, John Greenleaf Whittier, that Brown's execution had made " 'the gallows as venerable as the Cross!' "

Of the Confederate prisoners ("simple, bumpkin-like fellows ... with faces singularly vacant of meaning") then being held in the engine-house, Hawthorne observed with acute insight that nothing justified the war more than the possibility that Union victory might "free this class of southern whites from a thralldom in which they scarcely begin to be responsible beings."

He was not, anyway, entirely unsympathetic to the South, feeling toward "enemies" the kind of ambivalence (not unknown in twenty-first century America) born of the knowledge that men are brothers under the skin — a perception peculiarly appropriate to the War Between the States. Dual allegiances to nation and state (the last of which he believed was necessarily "nearest the heart"), Hawthorne understood, had "converted crowds of honest people into traitors, who seem to themselves not merely innocent, but patriotic, and who die for a bad cause with as quiet a conscience as if it were the best." Sympathetic, but not soft: "If a man loves his own state . . . and is content to be ruined with it, let us shoot him, if we can, but allow him an honorable burial in the soil he fights for."

On the other hand, encountering in northern Virginia a group of "contrabands" — escaped slaves — Hawthorne felt "most kindly" toward them, despite what appeared to him to be their "primeval simplicity." Presciently, Hawthorne concluded that whoever might most benefit from the war, "it will not be the present generation of negroes (sic), the childhood of whose race is now gone forever, and who must henceforth fight a hard battle with the world, on very unequal terms." Whether "freedom" would be worth fighting that battle was then and may still be debated, but Hawthorne's observation predated by several months the Emancipation Proclamation and accurately forecast the troubled near-century that would follow. As did his views on John Brown, moreover, his thoughts on the "contrabands" reflected the differences — existing even in wartime — between northern moderates and "Black Republican" abolitionists.

Hawthorne was farsighted, also, when allowed to inspect the *Monitor* ("a platform of iron, so nearly on a level with the water that the swash of the waves broke over it . . . it could not be called a vessel at all; it was a machine") shortly after its epochal defeat of the *Merrimack* — the first naval battle of ironclads. This "new war-fiend," he saw at once, though it looked like a "gigantic rat-trap . . . ugly, questionable . . . evidently mischievous," was destined to annihilate whole navies, "batter down old supremacies" and change the very practices of war, on land as on sea. "Already we hear of vessels the armament of which is to act entirely beneath the surface of the water;" indeed, "human strife is to be transferred from the heart and personality of man into cunning contrivances of machinery which by and by will fight out our wars with only the clank and smash of iron." The age of the MX and the guided missile lay inexorably, and not too far, beyond the *Monitor*.

Despite Fields's editorial pencil, the focus of Hawthorne's trip and his article were necessarily on the president (not then visible on any home screen, as all modern presidents are, relentlessly). The writer made a White House visit early one morning in company with a delegation that was to present Lincoln the ceremonial product of a Massachusetts whip factory. While waiting for the president to finish his breakfast, the group was joined by the secretaries of War (Stanton) and Treasury (Chase), and several unnamed others — "all with an equal right to look our head-servant in the face."

When Lincoln arrived, Hawthorne saw — a description Fields was to excise — "a tall, loose-jointed figure . . . whom (as being about the homeliest man I ever saw, yet by no means repulsive or disagreeable), it was impossible not to recognize as Uncle Abe." The sight caused him to wonder, as men contemplating the vagaries of American politics puzzle still about its workings, "that he, out of so many millions, unlooked for, unselected by any intelligible process . . . based upon his positive qualities, unknown to those who chose him, and unsuspected of what endowments may adapt him for his tremendous responsibility, should have found the way open for him to fling his lank personality into the chair of state — where, I presume, [he threw] his legs on the council-table and [told] the Cabinet Ministers a story." Lincoln seemed so true to "the pattern American" that Hawthorne felt that he already "had shaken hands with him a thousand times."

From that one quick meeting, Hawthorne the writer took the impressions that enabled him later to paint in words a picture of the ultimately martyred Lincoln that most Americans today — none of whom ever actually saw him — still carry in their hearts. The president's bushy hair was uncombed, he wore a "rusty" frock coat and slippers, his complexion was "dark and sallow," he had a big nose, thick eyebrows, sharply defined lines about his mouth — the whole "redeemed, illuminated, softened and brightened by a kindly though serious look out of his eyes" and a "homely sagacity that seems weighted with rich results of village experience."

Lincoln accepted the ornate gift-whip gracefully, "as an emblem of peace, not punishment," but Hawthorne was disappointed that he did not tell one of the "delectable stories" with which Washington was by then familiar — even though "they smack of frontier freedom and would not always bear repetition in a drawing-room, or on the immaculate page of the *Atlantic*." Editor Fields surely must have agreed with that last judgment.

Following the nineteenth-century custom, Hawthorne had given his essay the euphemistic byline "By a Peaceable Man." His exposure to war and soldiers, however, did not altogether bear out this pen name nor always produce his shrewdest observations. Like males in every age, he was often exhilarated by the military atmosphere; his nostrils seemed to dilate when he spied troops marching or officers on horseback — noting, for example, one of McClellan's aides, "a gallant cavalier, high-booted, with a revolver in his belt . . . a healthy hue of exposure and an expression of careless hardihood . . ."

Sometimes, Hawthorne wrote as if he were one of those "embedded" correspondents who, more than a century later, found themselves traveling with the American forces invading Iraq (and sometimes reported on these troops' progress or setbacks with the "editorial we"). The sight of that "high-booted" officer, for instance, set Hawthorne to gushing about the "good fortune" of young men who could take part in a war and share the "morally invigorating . . . atmosphere of the camp and the smoke of the battlefield." Sounding like Theodore Roosevelt at his worst, he wrote breathlessly of "the exhilarating sense of danger — to kill men blamelessly, or to be killed gloriously," in which the trappings of civilization vanished and men could follow "their native instincts of destruction."

Indeed they could, and did, in the Civil War and all combats before and since. But Hawthorne — perhaps as that pistol-packing officer rode out of sight — quickly regained his balance and "a peaceable man's" view of war and destruction. "When we measure our advances from barbarism," the author of *The Marble Faun* realized near the end of his journey of inspection, we "find ourselves just here" — not far along the road. "Set men face to face, with weapons in their hands, and they are as ready to slaughter one another now . . . as in the rudest ages, that . . . thought no wine so delicious as what they quaffed from an enemy's skull."

Back at the Wayside in Concord, after his brief immersion in the upheavals of war, Hawthorne took a vaguely apocalyptic view of what he had seen and experienced. He saw no alternative but "to go on winning victories," though he expressed no more confidence in real peace and a truer union in a future generation than he saw in the present. He even envisioned the possibility that the Confederates might win the war, but in that case, he suggested, the skies would not have fallen: "heaven was heaven still," as Milton had written after Lucifer and the angels seceded from "the golden palaces."

That conclusion was in the great — but too often flouted — tradition of the journalist as "no-sayer." That tradition is what distinguishes journalism, if rarely; kings and generals and politicians constantly say "yes, we can," but the journalist should, and sometimes does, say, "stop and think again" — sometimes even "no, we can't." Hawthorne probably never thought of himself as a journalist, anymore than did Hemingway or Steinbeck or any other reporter-turned-novelist,[2] the prestigious novel being still what Henry James called it: the "baggy monster" of truth and perception.

In his brief journey to the war, however, in his guise as "a peaceable man," Nathaniel Hawthorne was the best of journalists — even with his tendency sometimes to let appearance or assertion cloud his judgment, his occasional lapses into nineteenth-century verbosity. A modern journalist surely would do it more economically, come more directly to the point (if in the long run that matters to anyone but a newspaper editor). But he or she might well not have Hawthorne's eye for the telling detail (who needs it, with TV cameras always on hand?), or his curiosity about underlying truth or falsity beneath the ever-present "spin" — much less the ability and vocabulary to tell a story or picture a scene, such as a rumpled Lincoln receiving a ceremonial whip right after eating his breakfast. The modern journalist almost certainly would lack Hawthorne's sense of history and fallibility, and perhaps the vision to conceive of, certainly to concede, the least pleasant possibilities.

A perceptive, courageous and sharp-eyed writer — journalist or novelist — was rare and indispensable in Hawthorne's time, and no less so in ours. Having settled for the ubiquitous TV camera and the "embedded" reporter, the modern age may even be the poorer.

---

[1] The full text of Hawthorne's article is to be found on p. 127.

[2] When Robert Lowell called Norman Mailer the best journalist in America, Mailer replied that he thought he was the best writer in America.

The Wayside, Concord

Hawthorne's last home, Hillside, was purchased from Bronson Alcott. As it stood "too nigh, indeed" to the road, he renamed it The Wayside. After adding a library, bedroom and the tower-study at great expense, Hawthorne griped that he had "transformed a simple and small old-fashioned farmhouse into the absurdest anomaly you ever saw . . . If it would only burn down! But I have no such luck." The National Park Service maintains the site today.

Afterword

The last years of life remaining to Hawthorne were times of increasing weakness and failing health — his writing study towering above The Wayside homestead in Concord proved too hot in the summer and too cold in the winter. Characteristically, Hawthorne was often dissatisfied with his physical situation. He wrote of Salem that he came to dislike it "so much that I hate to go our into the streets, or to have people see me." Of the little red house in the Berkshires he complained it was "the most inconvenient and wretched little hovel that I ever put my head in…" But his final discomforts were mortal — part of the process of dying. Towards the end he wrote:

> Nobody ever suffered more from pens than I have, and I am glad
> that my labor with the abominable little tool is drawing to a close.[1]

His longtime friend and publisher, James T. Fields, who published *The Scarlet Letter* and shepherded his career with care and skill wrote reminiscences of authors he had known in 1883 — two decades after Hawthorne's death[2].

> I am sitting to-day opposite the likeness of the rarest genius
> America has given to literature, — a man who lately sojourned in
> this busy world of ours, but during many years of his life
> "Wandered lonely as a cloud," —
> a man who had, so to speak, a physical affinity with solitude.

One cannot know what Hawthorne might have said of this sentiment; he once commented on paintings, photographs and engravings of himself — a comment that seems to hold more meaning than perhaps was intended:

> In fact, there is no such thing as a true portrait; they are all

delusions; and I never saw any two alike, nor, hardly any two that I could recognize, merely by the portraits themselves, as being of the same man.[3]

———

Nathaniel Hawthorne's fame as a seminal force in American literature never faded — and that fame rewarded his talent far above the advances and royalties he earned during his lifetime. From the publishing of his short stories, to the novels and magazine articles, to the posthumous publication of his journals, he firmly endured as a star of American literature. As Brenda Wineapple noted: "He's given Americans and American authors a mirror though which they see their culture darkly and by which we, as Americans, have come to know ourselves and our nation — insofar as, Hawthorne suggests, this is ever possible."

Today, as America finds its international reputation questioned worldwide, many seek to define our historic values, our successes and compromises as the self-styled New World Eden. In this context it is well to remember the encounter between the aspiring young Ohio writer, William Dean Howells, who came East from what was then regarded as a cultural frontier to meet his heroes and mentors, the members of the New England intellectual and literary establishment, Hawthorne among them. Howells recounts how Hawthorne posed what Howells thought to be a telling inquiry of his visitor, namely, whether in the West, where American sensibility blended with unspoiled Nature, there was any place, in his experience, where the shadow of Puritanism hadn't fallen.

In seeking to understand our own creative ethos, this land of freedom and slavery, the literary legacy of the nineteenth century takes an important place along with the philosophy of the Founding Fathers of the eighteenth century and the political and social evolution of the twentieth. What our heritage will mean for the twenty-first — and whether the shadow of that Puritanical pedigree will darken our future — is an enigma that is our continuing destiny to explore.

— Gordon Hyatt & David Scribner

---

[1] *Letters*, Nathaniel Hawthorne, March 14, 1864, p. 648.
[2] *Yesterdays with Authors*, James T. Fields, Houghton Mifflin and Company, Boston, 1883, page 41.
[3] *The American Notebooks*, Page 491.

Contributors

LOUIS AUCHINCLOSS is a former president of the American Academy of Arts and Letters and the author of some sixty volumes of fiction and nonfiction.

PAUL AUSTER is the author of eleven novels, most recently *The Book of Illusions* and *Oracle Night*. He lives with his wife and daughter in Brooklyn.

LAURA L. BUTTERS has been Historic Site Manager of The Old Manse in Concord, Massachusetts, for The Trustees of Reservations for the past eight years. A native of Wisconsin, she received her bachelor of arts degree from the University of Wisconsin-Madison and a Graduate Certificate in Museum Studies from Harvard University.

M. GERARD FROMM, is a clinical psychologist on the staff of the Austen Riggs Center in Stockbridge, Massachusetts, where he directs the Center's Erikson Institute for Education and Research. He is also on the faculty of the Massachusetts Institute for Psychoanalysis.

WENDELL GARRETT is senior vice president of American Decorative Arts at Sotheby's, New York. For many years he was editor and publisher for *Antiques* magazine. Author of *The Worlds of Thomas Jefferson*, among other books, he is a writer of American social history. He lives in New York City.

CAROL GILLIGAN is the author of *In a Different Voice* and most recently, *The Birth of Pleasure*. Her adaptation of *The Scarlet Letter* was produced by Shakespeare & Company in 2002. She contributed to *110 Stories: New York Writes after September 11*, and teaches at New York University where she is a university professor.

MICHAEL T. GILMORE is the Paul Prosswimmer Professor of American Literature at Brandeis University.   His books include *American Romanticism and the Marketplace* (1985), *Differences in the Dark* (1998), and, most recently, *Surface and Depth* (2003).

ELIZABETH HARDWICK is a novelist and essayist. One of the founders of *The New York Review of Books*, her last book is a biography of Herman Melville. Ms. Hardwick lives in New York City.

HARRISON HAYFORD served as General Editor of the Northwestern-Newberry Edition of *The Writings of Herman Melville* from 1965 to 2001. With Merton M. Sealts Jr., he edited the landmark University of Chicago edition of *Billy Budd, Sailor* (1962).

NEIL HICKEY is editor-at-large of the Columbia Journalism Review. He is a lifelong journalist who has reported from Vietnam, the Soviet Union, the Persian Gulf, Eastern Europe, Northern Ireland, Cuba and elsewhere. He lives in New York.

GORDON HYATT, documentary film producer, has been involved in cultural and civic activities throughout his professional life. He served as Project Director of the 2000-2001 celebrations honoring Herman Melville's arrival in the Berkshires and the publication of *Moby-Dick* and the commemorative book *Aspects of Melville.* He originated this publication to honor the Hawthorne Bicentennial and is producer of the October 2004 celebration gala at Ozawa Hall. He lives in New York City and Stockbridge, Massachusetts.

ALEXANDRIA MASON has been the Curator at The House of the Seven Gables since 2001. She holds a bachelor of science degree in Historic Preservation from Roger Williams University and a masters degree in History from the University of St. Andrews in Scotland. While she is an avid Hawthorne enthusiast, her main goal as curator is to preserve Hawthorne's birthplace and The House of The Seven Gables so that generations to come may enjoy a tactile connection to this great author.

HERSHEL PARKER is the author of the two-volume *Herman Melville: A Biography*. Both volumes won top Association of American Publishers awards, the first (in 1997) in the category Literature and Language, the second (in 2003) in Biography and Autobiography. In 1997, the first volume was a Pulitzer Prize finalist. After Harrison Hayford's death, he became the General Editor (for the past two volumes) of the Northwestern-Newberry Edition of *The Writings of Herman Melville*. He lives in Morro Bay, California.

PEGGY STRONG received her bachelor of arts degree in English and American Studies from the University of Sussex, England and holds an masters degree from the State University of California, Fullerton. Her thesis, *Cross Currents of Culture and Character,* compares a character from Hawthorne's tale "My Kinsman Major Molineaux" with the young Ben Franklin in Franklin's *Autobiography.*

TOM WICKER began working for The New York Times in Washington in 1960, covering the White House, Congress and national politics. As White House correspondent in 1963, he was in Dallas with President Kennedy and subsequently covered Kennedy's assassination. He became chief of the Washington bureau in September 1964, and in 1966 began writing the "In the Nation" column for The Times' op-ed page. Wicker is the author of nine novels, among them *Unto this House* (1984), and *Easter Lilly* (1998), and six works of nonfiction, including *Kennedy without Tears* (1964), *On Press* (1978), *One of Us: Richard Nixon and the American Dream* (1991), and *Tragic Failure: Racial Integration in America* (1996).

BRENDA WINEAPPLE is a fellow of the John Simon Guggenheim Memorial Foundation and the American Council of Learned Societies, and was twice a fellow of the National Endowment for the Humanities. She is the author of *Genêt: A Biography of Janet Flanner* and *Sister Brother: Gertrude and Leo Stein,* and her essays and reviews appear in such national publications as the *New York Times Book Review, The Los Angeles Times, The American Scholar,* and *The Nation.* Her most recent book is *Hawthorne: A Life* (Alfred A. Knopf).